To KATHI

Ask away :)

You Don't Ask, You Don't Get

Proven Techniques to Get More Out of Life

Enjoy!

Janet F. Williams

You Don't Ask, You Don't Get
Proven Techniques to Get More Out of Life
by Janet F. Williams

Published by:
Good Day Media
P. O. Box 1007
San Marcos, CA 92079

www.GoodDayMedia.com
info@GoodDayMedia.com

Copyright 2010 by Janet F. Williams

Cover design by Michelle Livermore, Janet Elk and Janet F. Williams
Interior design by William Metcalfe

All rights reserved. No part of this work may be reproduced in any form by any means, electronic, mechanical, photographic or otherwise, including any type of recording, or be stored in an information storage or retrieval system, transmitted, or otherwise copied for public or private use, other than for "fair use" as brief quotations embodied in articles and reviews, without prior written permission from the publisher or author.

The author does not dispense medical advice or prescribe the use of any technique as a form of treatment for physical, emotional, or medical problems or conditions. Readers should seek their own advice and treatment from a physician or qualified professional. The suggestions contained in this book are for your information only. The publisher and author assume no responsibility for actions taken by others.

ISBN: 978-0-9844394-0-9
Williams, Janet F., 1955-
You Don't Ask, You Don't Get: Proven Techniques to Get More Out of Life / Janet F. Williams
      1. Self-help 2. Communication 3. Sales
      302

First printing 2010

Printed in the United States of America.

Dedication

To my sweetie.

You gave me the most precious gift of all – your love.

Notes and Acknowledgments

You Don't Ask, You Don't Get is full of real life stories, though not all are first-hand accounts. Stories are edited for brevity, all names are fictionalized, and some details may have been changed. I extend my sincere thanks to all who contributed. *You Don't Ask, You Don't Get* is more complete because of your input.

I've made an effort to use "he" and "she" with equality and a minimum of stereotyping. Spouse may mean partner or significant other.

I wish to acknowledge the help of my editors: Lois Winsen, Janet Elk and Julia Carson. Thank you very much. I've become a better writer with your support. I appreciate your patience and knowledgeable suggestions. I hope you receive at least as much as you have given.

Generous thanks go to Michelle Livermore and Janet Elk for their help with the book cover design, and to Bill Metcalfe for his book layout expertise.

This book is not intended to replace, advocate or offer advice on specific medical, psychological, financial, or other regulated professional issues and legalities as I am not a doctor, psychologist, lawyer, accountant, etc. Please take responsibility for your actions and employ proper professional assistance as needed.

Introduction:
Why You Need This Book

Do you want to get more out of life? *You Don't Ask, You Don't Get* is your guide to self-enrichment from small requests that maximize a moment to large requests capable of transformation. Now you can achieve more than you ever thought possible. Here's how:

This book will teach you:

- How to ask for what you want

- How to uncover the hidden motivators that make others want to grant your requests

- How to ask for things you never would have thought of on your own

- How to ask in specific situations

- How to overcome objections that stop you from asking for what you want

- How to overcome objections raised by others

Imagine being able to make a request of your spouse, boss, family, friends, salespeople, or anyone else, and get more of what you want in every aspect of your life. There are practice suggestions to help you put to use the information explained in this book.

It's fast and easy

You'll be shown how minor changes in the way you ask for things make a huge difference in the outcome. You'll find out how to create an atmosphere of giving so others are more prone to offer you more than you hoped to receive. You'll learn how to give to get. Each section of *You Don't Ask, You Don't Get* brims with examples and true stories relevant to everyday encounters, so you can understand how to apply these techniques to your life starting today!

Change a history of "No!" into a future filled with "Yes!"

You will be shown simple yet powerful techniques used by successful negotiators. You'll learn how to sell when making requests without sounding like a salesperson. You'll discover how to reach a decision-maker and when it's appropriate to step up the volume. In addition, you'll learn how to ask in specific situations. But more importantly, the information, tips and techniques contained inside this book will enable you to apply this knowledge in any situation.

Help yourself

You'll gain insight into why you don't ask for what you want and how to change your mindset for more positive results. There are sections devoted to overcoming objections – including your own. As you stretch and grow you'll gain confidence each time you refer to *You Don't Ask, You Don't Get* – a reliable source of inspiration.

Many wonderful folks hold themselves back because they were taught not to ask or didn't know what to say. Fears about reaching out kept them from living a rich life. It's sad when someone doesn't reach his or her full potential. You can't go back in time, but you can start asking for all kinds of things you never thought could be yours.

You've got to ask

Over the years, I've been in thousands of selling situations, sometimes as the buyer, other times as the seller. When recounting my tales, I can't tell you how many times someone commented, "I didn't know you could do that!" or "It never occurred to me to ask for that." They couldn't help but think of their own lost opportunities.

If you want something, you'd better ask for it because most situations don't call for giveaways, nor are people mind readers. You need to ask, and you need to ask in the right way to improve your chances of getting what you want. Will all your requests be answered favorably? Of course not. But you will have the knowledge to increase your chances by using the positive techniques contained in this book.

Honest, effective communication

Getting what you want out of life is important in order to live fully, and *You Don't Ask, You Don't Get* makes it easy to get what you want in a positive way. Forget negativity! You can ask and receive while maintaining your integrity. Focus on the positive and get a positive result. Everyone has inner motivations that drive thinking and action. You will learn how to uncover these hidden motivations so you can effectively deal with them. Include the right questions and you've created a winning combination to get what you want and give others what they want while exercising the core value of honesty.

Kindness, integrity and gratitude

Kindness and a good attitude work to your advantage. Personal rewards attained through kindness produce a feeling money can't buy. Kindness is like sharing a laugh – it feels good and spreads to those nearby. Like a warm blanket, your gratitude and thankfulness will wrap around those you help and those who help you.

When you stay true to yourself, you can look in the mirror each morning and like what you see because you're trying your best. Kindness is contagious. Use it to your benefit and you'll share the reward of getting the things important in your life while staying faithful to your integrity. You may never discover a medical cure, but you can leave a legacy that lives on through kind acts and ethical behavior.

Start a trend

Sure you ask for things, but it also feels wonderful to receive without having to ask. Be the person who gives before being asked and help start a trend. Your valuable gifts may have nothing to do with things. They may be about giving a gift of your time, talent, wisdom or love. You enrich your own life when you enrich the lives of others by giving of yourself kindly and freely. It is much easier to receive when you are the first to give.

There's nothing else like it

There are many fine self-help books devoted to personal growth, relationships and communication, and other manuals geared toward negotiating and salesmanship. *You Don't Ask, You Don't Get* spells out in simple terms how everyday folks can combine this material to further enrich their own lives. Prove it to yourself – *You Don't Ask, You Don't Get* helps you get where you want to go.

Spread the good word

Over time, use of the techniques in *You Don't Ask, You Don't Get* will add up to a life filled with more of what you want. After you experience your own successes, you'll be able to expand these concepts to fit naturally into your personal style. When your friends witness your newfound abundance and sense of fulfillment, they'll ask you what's different. Don't keep it to yourself. Tell them and share the wealth. It won't cost you a thing!

My favorite question

Here's a quick tip to get you started. It's a great question to use in almost any information gathering situation when you've reached a stopping point or aren't sure how to continue. Ask: "What haven't I asked that I would want to know?" This question opens doors you didn't know existed. Use it often. It works, as do the other invaluable tips and techniques you're about to discover in *You Don't Ask, You Don't Get.*

Table of Contents

What's In It For Me?

WIFM – What's In It For Me

You have an internal radio playing in your head. It's usually dialed down low, like background music behind the myriad thoughts that pass quickly through your mind. This radio has one station – WIFM – What's In it For Me. The messages on WIFM are part of your inner voice. You dial up the volume when compelled by various needs. This is not out of selfishness or because you're oblivious to anyone else's needs. You have to take care of yourself before you can effectively take care of others.

What's in it for them

Everyone is tuned in to their own WIFM station. If you think the secret to getting what you want is to get the other person to turn off their internal radio and tune into your WIFM frequency, you're wrong. A positive response to your request is based on the other person's WIFM motivations. That's why you need to discover what's in it for them to grant your request.

Crank up your volume with "I want! Gimme! Gimme!" and guess what you'll get? Nothing! Kids may be able to finagle a toy or ice-cream treat that way, but in general, annoying behavior will not get you what you want.

Intuitively you know your requests deal with a sense of balance or fairness even when they require little or no effort on another's part. When you want a big favor, chances are you'll need to throw in an enticement before anyone will agree to give you what you want. Turn the tables and the same is true.

WIFM static

Being tuned to WIFM does not make you self-centered, needy, greedy, or give you a sense of entitlement. You can listen to WIFM and not worry about impinging upon someone else's air space. You can give and receive as you normally do. In generous moments it's likely you do things for others "just because," without a hint of expectation and for no special or apparent reason.

Even altruistic behavior has its origins at the same radio station. So-called selfless giving through anonymous philanthropic contributions provides the warm satisfaction of doing a good deed by supporting a worthy cause. It promotes the giver's belief system of doing the right thing, even when giving is perceived as duty. An added bonus might be to witness the enjoyment of others as they receive gifts, or you might receive a nice income tax deduction. Someone else may receive the larger benefit in terms of material goods or services, but it's still a benefit for the giver. WIFM promotes both giving and receiving. It's only a negative when unbalanced.

Stay tuned to WIFM

Once you recognize WIFM is pervasive, you can begin to work with it and make it work for you. Ask yourself why anyone is going to give you what you want when they're interested in themselves. Their reasons will fit into one or more of the seven WIFM motivations explained in the next chapter.

The 7 WIFM Motivations

People give you what you want because they get something out of it. They may like you, it's convenient, they want to do something special for you, it's their job, they think it's the right thing to do, they have the tool you need, or for any number of reasons. You have your own reasons why you grant requests from others. All of them fall within the seven WIFM motivations listed below.

The 7 WIFM motivations
- Emotional
- Physical/Energy
- Logical
- Fairness
- Spiritual/Beliefs
- Personal
- Financial

Emotional WIFM
This motivation satisfies an emotional need for getting or giving love, warmth or friendship. It makes one feel special, superior, valued, important or powerful to oneself or others. It evokes happiness or other positive feelings. It reinforces one's sense of self whether positive or what we may perceive to be negative, including martyrdom, guilt, antipathy or even antisocial feelings.

Physical/Energy WIFM

This motivation brings food, sex, health, recreation, exercise, warmth, coolness, relaxation, sleep, or other sensations. It proves convenient or otherwise saves time or energy.

Logical WIFM

This motivation appeals to the logical side of the brain, allowing it to solve a problem where personal expertise can be demonstrated. In other words, it makes sense.

Spiritual/Beliefs WIFM

This motivation satisfies a spiritual or religious need, promotes a belief system, ethics, morals and/or values. It provides an opportunity to exercise or support those beliefs.

Fairness WIFM

This motivation appeals to a sense of fairness, balance or equality. There is an expectation to receive an amount equal to what is given, either now or later. It includes a sense of obligation to repay a favor or previous amount received, especially if one hasn't granted a request from the other lately, or did grant similarly weighted requests from other family members, co-workers or friends.

Personal WIFM

This motivation furthers personal goals or helps meet everyday responsibilities. It fits well with something one is trying to accomplish, for example in one's career or personal growth.

Financial WIFM

This motivation provides monetary or material value, aids productivity, improves sales figures and the like.

When you ask something of someone, your request and their response are both influenced by one or more of the seven motivational categories in each individual's WIFM. The same holds true when someone is making a request of you. You have your own reasons for why you give or wish to receive, and it is not necessary that your reasons match someone else's. The truth is, the more you can give someone what they want, the more you'll get what you want. And if you don't ask, you don't get!

WIFM motivations are important and will appear in numerous chapters. Bookmark this chapter now for future reference.

Reasons You Ask

You ask for something because you want it. You want a puppy, an explanation, the sale price on jeans, five minutes of someone's time, forgiveness, a raise, the best deal on a used car, better communication with your spouse, to use an expired coupon, advice, a trip to Puerto Vallarta, the same gift your sister got, a massage, two-for-one movie tickets, laughter, a plan for the future, sex, the senior discount, sobriety, a backstage pass, a marriage date, acceptance, to change your major to theater arts, a bologna sandwich… the list goes on and on. And that's just for you personally.

You also want to give blood, volunteer your time, listen to a friend's problems, give back to your community, babysit, recycle, serve on a committee, feed the homeless, tutor a child, donate to a worthy cause and encourage others to do the same. You have an idea of what you want and you go for it. You want, you ask. Maybe you get it. Your station is tuned to WIFM.

Asking is a step toward WIFM fulfillment

You have wants and needs. Not everything is given; you must work to get it. You tell yourself, "I need this thing" or "I want that." Sometimes you ask another for what you want and other times you ask yourself.

Example

Suppose you are thinking about owning a mountain bike and

you ask yourself if buying the bike is a good idea. Purchasing the bike (financial WIFM) and joining with your friends would make you feel good (emotional WIFM), and the exercise (physical/energy WIFM) would be great, too. However, you know the automatic window in your car needs repair (physical/energy and financial WIFM) and lately your work demands extra hours (physical/energy, personal and financial WIFM). The strength of the WIFM motivations determines whether or not you go for it.

Secondary gains

It's not unusual to have two WIFM categories in conflict. The strongest motivation wins out even if it has a negative attached to it. You lose something on one end, but ultimately you gain a separate advantage or secondary gain.

Example

You may not feel like making love with your partner (emotional and physical/energy WIFM), but you offer to do so to keep your relationship going (emotional and personal WIFM).

You may not want to break your diet (physical/energy and personal), yet you ask potential clients to a social engagement (personal and financial WIFM) at a club they like where you'll end up eating rich food and drinking alcohol (physical/energy WIFM) because you hope to land a new account (personal and financial WIFM).

As you can see, why you ask and how you decide may involve different WIFM motivations whether what you want is for you or someone else. The strengths of the various WIFM motivations influence and help you determine your decision.

Reasons You Don't Ask

The reason you don't ask for what you want is you believe WIFM is better served by holding off, except instead of delaying temporarily, you don't ask – ever! Making a request is a form of risk-taking. Self-talk helps you decide if the risk is worth the reward.

Policing yourself

You may feel that asking for something doesn't serve your best interests. Your WIFM motivations tell you to be careful, to hold back. The timing may not be right. Someone could get angry. You don't feel you have enough information, or the right words, or you don't want to risk embarrassment. There are a hundred reasons why you keep your mouth shut including avoiding obligation, shyness, your consideration for others, feelings of inadequacy, not wanting to hear the truth or a lie, or perhaps your request defies the chain of command, seems irrational or otherwise tests your sensibilities. In any case, your motivations to hold back are stronger than the ones that would propel you forward.

Breaking the habit

You may have been taught not to ask or thought you couldn't ask. The voice in your head could sound like a parent, spouse, friend, clergyman, teacher, or boss. Much of what you hear in your head was formed from past experience and reinforced through habit. Your self-talk could be based on outdated notions or messages short on value. Maybe its time to break the habit.

At the heart of the matter is you. You are the one who decides whether you can or cannot ask. *Could, should, ought* and *but* are censoring words coming into your self-talk from your old belief system. Listen as you use these words, whether aloud or in your head, and determine the source of the voice. Ask yourself whether the message is a habit worth questioning or if the message still has a basis for how you feel today.

The road never travelled

Never asking is like the trip you never took. You'll never know the amazing adventures you might have enjoyed. In addition to regrets tied to intentionally missed opportunities, there is always the possibility you never thought to ask in the first place. Your brain filtered out the question before it had a chance to form. This is another learned habit, one you can easily change. You can learn to think ahead, to ask for things you never would have considered previously.

The lesser of evils

Asking can be hard. It may seem less difficult to act rather than ask and risk the possibility the other person will respond negatively. Some act anyway, believing asking for forgiveness is a better option than asking for permission. In this instance, the short-term satisfaction of acting bears more weight than repercussions handed down from not asking. You act based on your motivations. WIFM wins again.

How to Ask for What You Want

Reactive vs. Proactive Responses

A situation arises and suddenly you have a question. It's easy to be caught unaware and blurt out the first thing that comes to mind. You may ask the wrong thing, the wrong person, or the emotion in your voice may reveal more than you'd like to show. You are reacting on impulse and making it harder to get what you want.

Sink or swim

The problem with many day-to-day communications is they are *reactive* instead of *proactive*. You don't stop and think much about what you are going to say, or why, or how. You just open your mouth and respond to the general flow of conversation. Throw in a little attitude and *ouch!* It's no wonder you feel frustrated with outcomes that don't go your way.

Yet with a little forethought, you can be the captain of your fate. Before you ask, consider the consequences. Take the lead in conversation and open the door for a more positive outcome. Know where you're going before you take the first step. Place your foot on the right path, not in your mouth.

Slow it down

When busy or distracted, you may grab on to what you think is the quick and easy road. Pauses my feel awkward and you may feel rushed. You react quickly by habit. By taking a moment to communicate your real desire, you have a better chance of getting a satisfactory result. A few seconds is all it takes. By practicing the techniques and tips in this book, your reactive responses will be better thought out and your proactive reaction time will increase.

Example

Pretend that after doing a little bit of research, you've purchased a product. Dissatisfied with its performance, you return the item where you bought it. The three examples below describe a similar situation, but contain important differences.

Example showing no preparation

You: "I bought this desk phone and I don't like it. Can I get my money back?"

Store: "I'm sorry it didn't work out. Do you have your receipt?"

You: "No. I don't know what I did with it."

Store: "Do you want to exchange this phone for another?"

You: "I don't know. I'll figure out what I want later."

Store: "We do carry this phone. Without a receipt we can issue a store credit."

You: "Okay."

Store: "Here you go. The store credit is on your new receipt."

What happened

Your lack of preparation did not take you very far. Why even bother going to the store? For the most part, it was effort wasted.

Example showing preparation

You: "I bought this phone and it has too much static."

Store: "Really? It shouldn't do that."

You: "I'd like to return it, but I don't have a receipt. If I exchange it, I might have the same problem. What do you suggest we do?"

Store: "We could issue you a store credit or you could trade up to something better."

You: "I picked this model because it was supposed to be a good one for the price. I wasn't expecting to pay more. How do I know another one won't have static?"

Store: "Hmmm. Did you plug it in near a microwave? That can cause static. Let's plug it in here and see what happens. Yes, I hear the static. I'll get a new box of this same phone and plug it in. Okay, great! No static. I'm sorry. You must have gotten a bad phone. Take this one."

You: "Thanks! If I get this one home and I hear static, will you give me my money back?"

Store: "Yes. Let me know. Thanks for your business."

What happened

Before you went to the store you had a good idea of what you wanted, either a telephone that worked properly or your money back. You've expressed this wish to the salesperson and indicated your desire for a better outcome. By enlisting the help of the salesperson, you leave the door open for solutions that could be better than your expectation. The salesperson could have offered a free or discounted upgrade, which you may have liked better than your original purchase. A good salesperson is trained to save the sale and keep the customer happy. In this case, you've essentially asked the salesperson to troubleshoot for you.

After interacting pleasantly, the barrier between two strangers begins to break down. The salesperson becomes willing to do something extra for the customer who would have to make an extra trip if there are further problems with the second product.

Should the conversation turn nasty on either end, those barriers thicken and the tendency to dig in your heels takes over. The result is that neither party wants to give an inch.

How to make things worse

Not You: "This phone sucks. I want my money back."

Store: "Do you have your receipt?"

Not You: "No."

Store: "How do we know you purchased it here?"

Not You: "Duh! If I bought it somewhere else, I'd go there."

Store: "We can give you a store credit, but first you'll have to show proof of purchase."

Not You: "See if I ever buy anything from you again!"

What happened

This customer was hostile from the start. Demands, not questions, were issued and little information was presented to help the situation. Efforts to dominate through sarcasm proved ineffective and put off the possibility of a satisfactory outcome. Fresh from the prior negative transaction, the salesperson moves on to the next customer – you. What will your interaction be like?

Practice

Think of a recent experience you had similar to one of the above examples. Were you fairly well prepared? Or, were there moments when you reacted ineffectively or felt defensive? Play out how advance preparation or a different attitude could have brought about a more positive outcome.

Yes/No and Open-Ended Questions

"Yes" or "No" questions have their place. They're what you ask when you want a definitive reply. This type of question can lead to more information, but can also be a conversation stopper. Open-ended questions are not answerable with "Yes" or "No." They probe for information. What you need to know will determine which style to use.

Yes!

Ask a question hoping for a "Yes" and get one – great! You can move in a forward direction. When you hear "Yes, but…," "Maybe," "I don't know," or "We'll see," it means the conversation has turned toward the WIFM of the person granting your request. There will be at least one objection to overcome. The other person wants more information first, a concession of some sort, or other factors need consideration. You must work out the details before you can progress. After further discussion you may wish to conclude your conversation with a yes/no question to emphasize finality, such as: "We're both in agreement, right?" or "Is there anything else?"

Example of a "Yes" response

You: "Honey, do you want to try that new Chinese restaurant tonight?"

Honey: "Yeah, sure."

You: "Great! I can be ready in ten minutes."

No!

You ask your question hoping for a positive response and hear "No." What happens next? Convincing? Whining? Sweet talk? Anger? Coercion? The silent treatment? Bargaining? If any of these techniques push the other person to change his or her mind, you both pay a price. The rejection factor from hearing "No" may make you back off. You could try finding out what would change a "No" to a "Yes." Or, you could do nothing and get nothing.

Example of a "No" response

You: "Honey, do you want to try that new Chinese restaurant tonight?"

Honey: "No, not really."

Hearing "No" puts you one step backward. Now you're working from a deficit. Coming from behind takes extra effort. Improve your position before you begin.

How you phrase questions is partially a matter of habit. Yes/no questions typically start using one of these forms: *Do you..., May I..., Will you..., Is there..., Could he... Would she... Should I..., Are you..., Can they....,* and so on. Practice using these beginnings and listen to how your question forms.

Not everyone you meet is a stickler for how you word your question. When you ask the attendant at a movie theater if there is a student discount, he will skip the formalities and ask for your school ID.

For years I worked as a finance manager at automotive dealerships. It was typical to mark up the interest rate charged on both retail and lease contracts as a source of income whenever possible. When customers asked if I would negotiate the finance rate with them, my stock answer was "No." It was not in the company's best interest to continue negotiations after the sale terms had been agreed upon and this answer stopped further discussion. Was it negotiable? Occasionally. Under narrow circumstances I could and would negotiate the rate. It was their financial WIFM versus mine and the company's. A better approach for the customer would have been a question that invited information – an open-ended question posed during negotiations with the salesperson.

Open wide!

Do not ask a yes/no question unless you are prepared to accept the answer. Otherwise substitute an open-ended question. An open-ended question is just as it sounds – an invitation for the other person to reply as they see fit, one in which you are not asking for a simple "Yes" or "No." Open-ended questions engage the other person. You will hear a longer answer because you are asking for more information.

Open-ended questions open up possibilities. Preparation is key, so think ahead about what you want in your answer. Good open-ended questions start with either *who, what, where, when, why, how* or *which*. Practice a few questions beginning with these words and listen to the type of answers that naturally follow.

Examples of open-ended questions

You: "Hey, Honey, I'm in the mood for something different for dinner. Which restaurant do you think makes the best fish and chips?"

Honey: "Gary's Grill and Pub, no doubt about it."

You: "You are so right. Let's go there."

In sales lingo, "Let's go there," is an assumptive close. Honey can still protest, but chances are good this is a win-win.

You: "If you could have whatever you want to eat tonight, what would it be?"
Honey: "I guess I could go for some ribs."
You: "And I could go for fish and chips. Let's eat out."

Congratulations! You've inspired Honey to think beyond the refrigerator.

Take a few seconds to consider possible answers to your questions before you ask. In the examples above, Honey didn't have to be concerned with what was in the fridge and you were able to clarify what you want.

Ask the right question

When you want a specific type of answer, ask the right question and ask it the right way. Don't expect others to read your mind. First determine what you want. Ask for what you want in a way most conducive to reaching your desired outcome. Know your audience and consider your timing.

In a retail setting, you may not know your audience beyond the fact that you are working with a salesperson you hope is helpful. Your salesperson is probably going to answer the question you ask subject to his or her interpretation, and may not offer up the core information you seek.

A common shopping objective is to save money on purchases. The example below illustrates the differences in how you ask for something and the potential results. Each yes/no question and answer is followed by an open-ended question stating your more accurate objective – getting a deal – and a more accurate answer.

Example

You: "Do you have any bagels on sale?"
Store: "No, they're all the same price."
You: "What are today's specials?"
Store: "Buy a dozen bagels and get two free."

You: "Can I get a discount on this shelf unit?"
Store: "No."
You: "Which items qualify for a discount?"
Store: "We have a floor model I can discount."

You: "Are you able to give me a sale price on this similar item?"
Store: "No."
You: "Who can authorize the sale price on this similar item?"
Store: "My manager can approve non-sale item discounts."

You: "Are you having any sales?"
Store: "No."
You: "What kind of savings can you offer?"
Store: "I can take 20% off discontinued items."

You: "Are any of these items on sale?"
Store: "No."
You: "Where can I find your sale items?"
Store: "We have a clearance section in the back corner."

You: "Is your store credit card interest rate the same as a regular credit card?"

Store: "Yes."

You: "Why should I use your store credit?"

Store: "We offer three months with no interest."

Don't count on your salesperson to second-guess your intention. Ask for what you really want. Open-ended questions direct others to reply with thoughtful answers. Specific yes/no questions can nail down your answer, but on the other hand your assumptions may lead you off track. As the examples above illustrate, there is a difference between asking if something is on sale and asking how you can save money on your purchase. Be proactive and discern your real objective before you ask.

Practice

Think of a few yes/no questions. Now change them into open-ended questions by substituting *who, what, where, when, why, how* and *which*. Listen to the difference in the answer.

Using Assumptions to Your Advantage

In the last chapter, perhaps you noticed that assumptions can creep into your questions. Assumptions bias the outcome of the answer. This can help your request or work against you. Now you'll learn how to make assumptions work for you.

A shot in the dark

An assumption is like a guess, which may or may not be correct. Every time you make an assumption there is some risk you're off target because you don't have all the information you need to determine the whole truth. Your false assumption may lead you away from your desired destination and leave you with a reply or outcome you don't anticipate or want.

Example

"May I speak to your manager?"

This is specific, but you assume the manager is the person you need. You could end up wasting your time and the manager's.

The good news

On the other hand, assumptions can be used as a shortcut to success. You can use an assumption to lead the other person toward your goal by posing your question properly.

Example

"Who has the authority to remove this charge from my bill?"

This is what you want to know. You assume the charge can be removed from your bill and there is a person who can help you move forward with this task.

There are many ways to ask for what you want, but be aware that slight differences in the wording can change the meaning. You will get a better result by adding a qualifying word or phrase to a yes/no question that makes it more specific. The four questions in the next example all ask for the same thing – to fix a lamp. Note the differences in the question and the answer. The first two ask a yes/no question. The third asks a yes/no question with a qualifier. The forth is an open-ended question.

Example

"Can you fix the lamp?"

This asks if the person is able to fix the lamp.

"Will you fix the lamp?"

This question only covers intent. Then what?

"Can you fix the lamp today?"

Assumes the other person knows how to fix the lamp, and by adding the qualifier "today" asks when it will get done.

"What do you need to start fixing the lamp today?"

Assumes the other person knows how to fix the lamp and makes them think about how to get started on it right away. This question covers a lot of ground and includes the assumption that the other person will be doing the job.

As you can see, slight changes in how you word your question give you a slight advantage. Take away the choice of a "Yes" or "No" answer. Replace it with an assumption that helps the other person understand your objective. It moves their thinking away from an answer you may not want, to one that fits your preferred goal.

Example

"Will you forgive me?"

    You may not want to hear the answer to this question.

"How can I earn your forgiveness?"

    The wording assumes you can be forgiven. It's now just a matter of what you need to do to earn their forgiveness – a crucial distinction.

Assumption and risk

No matter how small, there is a risk when you use an assumption because guesses can be inaccurate. Even a non-self-serving gesture might bring about a reply you don't anticipate.

Example

"Do you need help?"

    Helping another is generally welcomed, but not always. Instead of hearing a pleasant, "Yes, thanks," you may hear a defensive, "Does it look like I need help?" or, "No! I can do it myself." Your question might be misinterpreted by the other person. In the first negative reply the respondent makes an assumption that you think they're incompetent; in the second, that they are needy when you are only wondering if you could somehow be of service with no thought of being judgmental. Your tone of voice conveys part of your message. Others pick up on your attitude and interpret that, as well.

"How can I help you?"

This changes the yes/no format to an open-ended question. The other person may still vent their frustration at what they perceive to be your negative assumption about them, or they may jump past their ego and get to the problem area.

"Why don't I bring a casserole tomorrow night so your family doesn't have to cook?"

In this case your suggestion bypasses if or how you might help by offering a specific solution that the other person may accept or decline. No matter the answer, you assume your well-meaning offer will be appreciated during a time when the other person may not have the presence of mind to come up with how you might help.

Know it all? Not at all

How many times have you had a question or wanted something but didn't ask because you assumed you knew the answer? Unless you're lucky, this assumption either gets you nowhere or gets you in trouble – take your pick. Let's see, you didn't buy the suit you wanted because you assumed you had already spent too much of your yearly clothing budget. You didn't ask for a hot air balloon ride for your birthday because you assumed your husband would freak out. You didn't take your briefcase to the lunch meeting because you assumed your client's issues weren't on the agenda. You assumed your wife would pick up the dog food because she was out running errands. Not everyone thinks as you do. You don't know what's on another person's mind and to believe you do is an assumption that doesn't work in your favor. For better results, don't assume; ask!

The woman in the next story made numerous assumptions and did not bother to clarify them for reasons related to several of her WIFM motivations. In hindsight, she wished she had asked.

As a teen-ager, Carol ran with a rough crowd from the poor side of town. One day she invited a few friends to her house located in a better neighborhood. The guys got out of control and rifled through her parents' dresser drawers. She didn't see them take anything. However, at school a week later one of the guys was wearing an expensive watch she thought she recognized as belonging to her father. She confronted the boy. He denied taking the watch, but she assumed he had because how else would a nice older watch like that end up on this boy's wrist?

Scared of the repercussions of involving her father with these toughs and the prospect of being grounded, Carol silently carried her secret. Her father wore an inexpensive watch to work and she assumed he either didn't know the heirloom was missing or never thought to ask her what happened to it. Decades passed. Finally, after carrying her guilt for over thirty years, Carol asked her father if he ever wondered what happened to the old missing watch and told him the story. He informed her she was mistaken. Years ago he had put the watch in a safe deposit box. He later gave her the key.

People are not mind readers

You cannot assume others have all the information or are mind readers. To do so will yield disappointment in your unmet expectation. Explaining particulars helps others provide you with what you need. Here's a common scenario: You go to an automotive shop and ask for what seems like a simple repair only to end up with a barrage of questions. This is not because the mechanic is dense or is intentionally trying to annoy you. It's because he doesn't have enough information. Speak up. By helping him you are helping yourself.

Be open to alternatives

Your assumptive question may limit appropriate answers by implying things have to be done a certain way when you may not be aware of better options. Be open to alternatives. People who have all the answers don't always match them up to the right questions!

Practice

Think of a question or two you've asked recently that included an assumption. What was the outcome? Write out how you would change your question should the situation arise again.

Who, What, Where, When, Why Plus How and Which

Kids in grade school are taught to give and receive information by identifying the 5 Ws: *who, what, where, when,* and *why*. It's a basic formula found inside a birthday party invitation and also the first few lines of a breaking news story. Less significant details come afterward.

The 5 Ws are incredibly important to your requests. You will save yourself a lot of time and energy when your request includes the best combination of who, what, where, when, and why. The list of 5 Ws can be expanded to include *how* and *which*. When your WIFM motivations drive you to ask for something, consider the five Ws when making your request.

Who

Who you ask may seem obvious. You ask the people involved, or you ask the salesperson standing in front you. Military personnel need to follow protocol. Asking the wrong person could result in unwelcome consequences. The same holds true at work. You need a decision-maker, but going to your boss's boss is usually not in your best interest.

Not all situations are easy to figure out when deciding whom to ask. Making an assumption can throw you off track or even backfire. It makes sense to do a little research, either on your own or by asking to find out who the best person is to hear your request.

Good *who* questions

- "Who is the best person to resolve this issue?"
- "Who will return my call?"
- "Who's available to help me?"

Years ago, when he was a young TV reporter, Ed's producer gave him an assignment to get a story about the new slow growth movement in the community. Ed went to every city councilman and every one of them turned down his request for an interview. Not only was he concerned about feeling foolish for not knowing his subject matter, he didn't want to bother the only other person who might help out – the mayor. With nowhere else to turn, Ed took a chance and contacted the mayor. He was astonished at the warm response he received and was able to set up the cameras to film Pete Wilson, then Mayor of San Diego, to get his story.

What

Want to know what's what? Stick to the subject. Imagine hearing this request: "Hey, I was wondering what you thought about a trip to the water park. The older kids will be out of school on Monday, Junior has soccer on Tuesday, and he won't go without his buddy, Tyler. We can switch cars if we need the room. What do you think?" Huh? It's going to take more than a few questions to untangle this mess. What was asked? Are you invited? What day is the trip? How many people are going? Time to revisit the 5 Ws.

Here's what's what

To get a clear answer, ask a clear question. Think: what do you want? Next, break up a long request into manageable parts. Asking for too much information all at once is confusing and puts people off. Give enough information up front to remove the obvious questions or objections the other person might have without giving a lengthy speech. Long explanations are tiresome to those used to today's quick text communication style.

Good *what* questions
- "What are my options?"
- "What would I want to know that I haven't already asked?"
- "What serves the greatest good?"

Where
Your immediate environment can have a strong impact, sometimes more than the words you choose. Just ask a guy who is ready to propose how much he's thought about where he'll pop the question. The right place becomes part of a story the couple will tell to their children and grandchildren.

Spontaneous requests occur wherever you happen to be at the moment. Where you ask doesn't always influence the answer. If location has a bearing, be sure to include where you'll ask when planning ahead.

Good *where* questions
- "Where are we at with this project?"
- "Where am I headed in life?"
- "Where can I find the information booth?"

When
Timing may not be everything, but it sure helps to know when it's a good time to ask. Consider your WIFM motivations. You may

have a deadline or your moment will pass. Plan ahead. Then make time to follow through with your preparations so that when the right time does present itself, you'll be ready.

Also, consider the other person's WIFM motivations. Some people like surprises and spontaneity, while others prefer to plan well in advance. Take advantage of how timing can add positive sparkle to your request. Somber emotions may go over better with a chosen moment, though sudden tragic situations give you fewer options.

You may have someone you rely on for a recurring request. That's great, but all it takes is one assumption or poor timing for you to realize you didn't ask soon enough and now you've lost out.

That's what happened to friends, Jordan and Deanna, who had a standing agreement to watch the other's cat when either of them went out of town. A few days before a trip, Jordan called Deana to ask when he could drop off his cat and Deanna informed him she was hoping to do the same. Their trips overlapped, forcing each to make last minute arrangements. Jordan found someone to come in and feed his cat, but the sitter proved not to be entirely reliable. Deanna ended up boarding her cat, an option she hoped to avoid.

Good *when* questions

- "When is a good time to discuss this?"
- "When can I expect to see results?"
- "When will I make time for myself?"

Why

You don't ask, you don't get!

Good *why* questions

- "Why do I spend money I don't have?"

- "Why does my store receipt say one thing and this sign says another?"

- "Why do you recommend these brake pads over the ones that came with the car?"

How

How you ask is wide-open territory. Consider WIFM for both parties and you've made a start. You can be direct, somewhat indirect, or so completely indirect you remove yourself and ask someone to ask for you. Your method can be emotional, logical, spiritual, or physical. You can ask softly or announce your request to the world. You can ask for little bits at a time or everything at once. You can ask with humor or pathos. You can plead. You can ask over a glass of wine or over the Internet. You can call, write, text, tweet or send a video. There are endless ways to communicate, and therefore, there are endless ways to ask.

Good *how* questions

- "How have you dealt with this issue in the past?"

- "How can I volunteer my services?"

- "How can I extend my payments on this bill?"

Which

You have choices. Choices are options, and options are good. They provide a measure of freedom or at least a little wiggle room.

Because you have choices, you aren't locked in to one way of doing or being or asking. You may not like your choices or you could be overjoyed at all the wonderful options at your disposal. You can choose which person you ask, which place you ask, which time you ask, and so forth. When deciding which way to go in forming your request, narrow it down to the best few choices. When you think you have all of them, challenge yourself to come up with a few more to keep from getting locked in to old ways of thinking.

Good *which* questions

- "Which route is more scenic?"
- "Which is better for my child's health?"
- "Which would you choose?"

Add it all together and you get...

While working on my post-graduate studies, I was tasked (why) with interviewing someone in the health field. I wanted to select (which) someone who would add interest to a potentially dry subject. I chose Robert Graham, (who), founder of the Repository for Germinal Choice, a.k.a. the "Nobel sperm bank," in part because he was a fellow Mensa member and I hoped that connection would be sufficient for him to grant me an interview. It wasn't too hard to find the phone number for the sperm bank and I gave him a call (how) before my paper was due. I explained why I was calling and asked for an interview (what). He agreed. The sperm bank (where) was within driving distance and we arranged a time to meet (when). It was truly a fascinating hour and I was able to translate that excitement when presenting my oral report.

Asking Tips and Techniques

You already know how to take situational advantage when you ask for something. You wait until your home team has won the game on TV before asking your husband for a favor. You ask Mom for date money instead of Dad because she likes your girlfriend better. You ask your roommate to drive because she'll use any excuse to take out her new car. When you know more about the psychology of asking, you'll know success more often.

Know your audience

The more you know the person answering your request, the better you can key into their WIFM motivations. Get to know the person ahead of time and be observant. Enlist the help of mutual friends or co-workers and ask them what the person is like. Take a few minutes to research their name or organization on the Internet.

Example

Suppose you want to take a personal financial class one day a week. The class time will impinge upon your workday by a couple of hours that you are willing to make up. Your boss, Mr. Jones, has the authority to approve or decline your request.

The better you know your boss, the easier it will be for you to ask for time off. You already know more than you think. Mr. Jones doesn't like being bothered in the morning before he's had his coffee and had a chance to check his e-mail. By mid-morning, his sense of humor kicks in. He eats lunch at his desk. A closed door means stay out, otherwise you're free to come in and talk. When he's on the phone he will never let you interrupt, nor will he acknowledge your presence when his boss is in his office. In the hallway, he walks fast so no one can stop him. At the end of the day, he talks about his family and pets. Everything you need to know is there.

Whom to ask

There are times when more than one person may be able to grant your request. Person A might help you out, but take forever to do it. Person B might also be willing to help, though it could cost you financially. Person C might be fast, but sloppy. You'll want to go to the person most likely to meet your most pressing need. Your WIFM motivations help you prioritize. Occasionally you may need to ask whom to ask.

On the home front, pick a sibling you believe is aligned with your sympathies or shares complementary WIFM motivations. At some point in time, most kids learn how to play Mom against Dad to get what they want. You know your good friends well enough to know whom to ask among them for various things.

At work, don't jump too far up the ladder. Asking a supervisor is a no-no when you should have asked your immediate boss. Going over your boss's head could cause you headaches in the long run.

Example

Mr. Jones is your immediate boss and has authority over your work hours. He's a natural to go to for your request. There's no need to go to anyone else. Should he decline your request, you would be wise to try to overcome his objections rather than talk to his superior or other higher-up.

When to ask

Make your request at a good moment for both you and the other person. Etiquette and respect for another's time is always appreciated no matter how familiar your relationship. Plan ahead and set aside a specific time to talk. Waiting until the last minute leaves you at the mercy of whatever else is going on. Unexpected schedule changes could mean you don't get a hearing or another chance. Purposely waiting for the last minute as a manipulative ploy to force an issue is not a good call. While you may get what you want, later you will pay a heavy price.

Example

Now, back to Mr. Jones. Bring up the subject of taking adult classes, so he is aware of your interest. Several weeks before the class, check in with him to be sure he's in a receptive mood. Beginning in the late morning you'll have several opportunities to talk in his office as long as no one else is around, or any time after lunch provided you get to him before he mentally checks out for the day. Courtesy counts. Approach Mr. Jones during a slow time in your day or when you're on break. He may not appreciate you taking time during normal business hours to discuss your personal plans when you are supposed to be focused on a tight deadline.

Where you ask

Where you make your request will have a psychological component. As mentioned previously, a guy ready to propose to his ladylove is getting ready for the right moment and place. It could be in front of a crackling fire, on a mountaintop or in the middle of a roller coaster ride. He's hoping he knows her well enough to choose an environment where she'll eagerly say, "Yes!"

At work, private conversations are best taken outside of common areas. Find a conference room, lounge, restaurant, media center, etc., where the ambient sound and lighting are favorable and there are few or no other ears to pick up gossip. Plan ahead and create the right environment.

Example

You'll probably be asking Mr. Jones about your class somewhere within the walls of the work environment. His office is his turf and your office or cubicle is yours. Determine which locale offers an advantage. A sudden opportunity might mean asking where you happen to be at the moment.

What you say

The words you choose are important. They make your case. Knowing your audience helps determine which words you select – words the other person will understand or relate to. Keep your conversation short and explain your request clearly. You may know what you're talking about, but that doesn't mean someone else will. Add in a little background information to avoid confusion. Use words that convey both your WIFM motivations and those of the other person.

Example

Remind Mr. Jones of your interest in personal finance. Inform him you have an opportunity to take a class and tell him about it using the 5 Ws. Let him know you are willing to be flexible about working extra hours to give your company back the time you will be spending in class. Be prepared to give to get. Include a legitimate reason why it would be beneficial for him to let you out of work to take the class. Remember, that's his WIFM motivation for saying "Yes."

How you say it

Your tone of voice carries meaning beyond the words you choose. Knowing your audience will help determine your delivery. Will you be businesslike? Emotional? Enthusiastic? Indifferent? Angry? Passion for your subject helps others feel your passion. If you sound as if you don't care, why would anyone else?

Facial expressions and body language provide other clues that get your message across. Practice in front of a mirror to be sure your body language matches what you say. Looking down, shuffling your feet and letting your arms hang limply at your sides when you make a request does not inspire a "Yes" response.

Example

Dress nicely and arrive for work on time the day you decide to ask Mr. Jones. Express a level of excitement when telling him about the class. Emotion in your voice helps him better understand and relate to your desire. Bring a colorful brochure or web page printout to visually reinforce your words. Your body language should match what you say so you can telegraph an overall look with confidence.

Give them what they want

By now you should be able to identify the WIFM motivations influencing you to ask for what you want. Before you make your request, write out a list of what you believe is the other person's WIFM. Be honest with yourself and exercise good judgment to increase your chances for success. The more you can give the other person what they want, the more likely it is you will get what you want.

Example

Mr. Jones believes happy employees are more productive, and having effective producers in his department not only gives him personal satisfaction (emotional, beliefs WIFM), but makes him look good when production figures come out (logical, personal, financial WIFM). Your new financial skills may have a business application (financial, logical WIFM). Find a tie-in ahead of time for how your class will benefit at work and Mr. Jones's department may pick up the tab (financial, logical, fairness WIFM).

Imagine how you would respond

Using the 5 Ws is a good reminder of the factors that come into play when you want something. Use them to tie in to WIFM when planning your request. Then, imagine you are asking yourself for the thing you will ask of someone else. How would you reply?

Practice

The next time you ask for something, review this chapter and compare how many asking tips you used. Identify the ones you used without first thinking about them. The others will come to you more quickly with forethought and practice.

Verbal and Visual Tips and Techniques

The words you use are only part of your message. Your delivery – tone of voice, emphasis and emotion convey more. Include body language to round out your presentation. You've heard the expression: "It's not what you say. It's how you say it." To that add: "It's not what you ask. It's how you ask it!"

Who's listening

When you ask for something from Tom you ask one way. When you ask something from Mary you ask it another way. Why? Because Tom and Mary are different and you tailor your request to connect with them as individuals. Tom likes things to the point, so you keep your conversation and requests short and sweet. Mary likes to linger on detail. She'll listen to a drawn out story or request. Don't expect a long answer from Tom. Don't expect a short answer from Mary.

The secret to your secret

In the right environment, a soft voice can make it seem like you're letting someone in on a secret. Start to whisper and ears perk up. In the wrong environment, you may come across as timid or unconvincing. The other person may not hear you against loud music or other background noise.

Example

You're in a crowded bar and after a few dances you want to ask your dance partner to go someplace where you can be together. Don't shout your private message. Keep it intimate. Take that person aside and lean in a little before asking if s/he wouldn't prefer a more quiet setting. Your body language should subtly reinforce your meaning.

Say it like you mean it

Confidence is catching. It helps the other person believe in your convictions and empathize with you. The more you can engage the other, the more likely you are to impress the importance of your request. Enthusiasm is also contagious. Show passion and ratchet up the life in your voice to elicit excitement. For full effect, bring enthusiasm into your gestures. To project more fully, sit up or stand before speaking. Smile when you talk and others will hear the happiness in your voice. These actions make you look and sound bright and alert. Above all, be sincere.

Example

"How about going to Lucky's Pizza instead? They've got an awesome new menu with wood-fired pizza. I hear their portobello calzone is to die for! Let's try it!"

Fire! Fire!

Your urgent tone speaks to immediate action, but it should only be used in a true emergency or time crunch. Others won't appreciate being rushed because of poor planning on your part. Do this a few times and you've created lack of trust that pushes others away from wanting to help. Ask for help ahead of time instead of asking for forgiveness, even on a short time line.

Example

"I've researched the companies able to patch the roof over the employee lunchroom. ABC Roofing can do a temporary fix over the small area. However, they have a break in their schedule and can fix the underlying problem of the overall slant for the whole 20' x 30' section. They'll do the job at a fifteen percent discount, but I need to call them today. Of course it will cost more than patching, but it's a great savings, especially when you consider we won't have to revisit this problem again. Here's their estimate. Can I give them your approval?"

Sell the sizzle

Use words that entice. Think of advertisements. Marketers know better than to say, "Buy our burgers. They're good." They carefully choose words to make your mouth water – succulent, juicy, tasty, delicious, scrumptious, gotta-have-it-can't-wait-another-second-unbelievably-fabulous! Add in the five senses as much as possible to make your point, and sell the sizzle as well as the steak.

Example

"Look at this idyllic picture of the cabin. Can't you just smell the flowers and hear the wind in the pines? I bet we could even drink the snow melt. We'll be so relaxed, we'll never want to leave! What do you say – shall we rent it for a week?"

Pacing

Matching someone's style of speaking, body language or behavior is called pacing. Pacing makes the other party feel you are fully in sync with them. Speak and gesture in ways similar to the person you're talking to, and you send out the message, "We're two of a kind." The other person picks up on this at an unconscious level. It helps you relate and establishes rapport. Obviously, you aren't going to imitate another person's lisp or foreign accent, or do something that might be interpreted as mocking.

Adopt the style of your surroundings. At the office this means wearing clothes similar to or better than co-workers in similar jobs.

Be businesslike and serious in a serious, businesslike office. You can joke around a bit if your boss likes to joke around. If she talks slower, you talk slower. If she leans in a little (a good sign), you lean in a little. At social gatherings dress and act to fit in or you'll be seen as not belonging. It's okay to want to stand out from the crowd and you can do this through small changes in dress or affect. Being boisterous when others are quiet, or wearing an evening gown when others are wearing shorts will certainly get you noticed, but not in a good way.

Pacing is subtle and natural, not a call to "look at me!" It helps others think of you as a peer, someone they can relax around. This added level of comfort leads to a better chance at success.

Example

You have new guests in your home. You bring out drinks and offer a few snacks. They speak softly, you speak softly. During conversation the man sets down his drink and crosses his ankle over his knee. You do the same. Later, he sits up and leans forward. You do the same. Don't be surprised to see your guests unconsciously mimicking you! Change your posture and see if one of them follows what you do. You are leading at this point – a good time to make a request, especially in a business situation.

R-E-S-P-E-C-T

Even when you meet someone for the first time, you may know quite a bit about them. The other person's title is an immediate clue – sales associate, manager, accounts payable clerk, doctor – as is the way they're dressed. It can be tempting to rush to judgment based on title or appearance. Before you get too involved, ask whether the person has the authority to handle your request. Be considerate. Show respect to a fellow human being and don't talk down to an employee you assume is an underling. Disrespect doesn't get you what you want. For all you know you're talking to the boss's daughter. Or, she could be the boss!

For a short time, I sold cars at a luxury import dealership. The regular sales staff typically ignored folks who wandered onto the lot if they didn't look like money. One day I approached a twenty-something young man and his lady friend who looked like they could barely pay the insurance on his beater. They didn't know what they could afford and asked for my help. They left with two new cars that night, a full-sized sedan and a cute demo that together totaled $100,000. The customers, the dealership and I were very happy with that outcome.

When you're here and they're there

You can't always make your request in person, which means you can't read or pace the other person's body language. On the phone your voice alone must carry the message. You may wish to learn the lingo of a specific trade to give the impression you are well-versed and knowledgeable on the subject relating to your request. This builds respect and credibility, and helps you establish rapport. The more you know, the closer you are to a solution. Sounding uninformed can make you an outsider and be the reason you don't get what you want.

Memos and e-mails take the place of what were formerly face-to-face encounters. Both are short missives, not long letters. Terse requests can come across as snippy or abrupt. Adding pleasantries like "please" and "thank you" (or "pls" and "tx") can make the difference. Never type in capital letters; it looks like shouting. Formal requests belong on stationery.

Hello, India?

You pick up the phone and call customer service – in India (or wherever). They don't know you and you don't know them. You still have some basic verbal clues to rely upon in your non-face-to-face interaction. Standard business protocol dictates people behave politely unless you give them a reason not to. Even then, company policy may not allow for anything else. When your best efforts don't get what you want, ask the customer service rep for the individual one up on the chain of command or a recommendation for the right person with whom to speak. Customer service reps are graded on calls. Let them know you were very happy with the level of service you received thus far even though you still have some unresolved issues, and you will have a better chance at talking to their supervisor. Otherwise, you may find yourself disconnected. Your voice is the only link to getting what you want. Make it work for you.

Avoid asking while impaired

Avoid making a request when you are drunk or otherwise impaired. You may not even remember what you asked and the other person may try to hold you to your end of the deal. You cannot make a good decision when you're not in a proper frame of mind. Your WIFM will be temporarily skewed by your altered mood or impaired health. Alcohol depresses your self-talk filter and depending on how much you drink, you might find yourself saying all kinds of things you wouldn't have while sober. Wait until you can make a reasoned decision, one that works in your favor, not to your detriment.

Practice

The next time you have friends or family in your home, try pacing their gestures and see who leads. Note the body language and words your guests use when they ask you for something. Take away what you find effective for your own use.

Ways to Ask

How should you ask? Let me count the ways. Select methods that key into strong WIFM motivations – yours, so you can convey confidence and enthusiasm for what you want and believe in, and theirs, so they'll have good reasons for wanting to grant your request. Choose a logical approach with a logical person and an emotional approach with an emotional person, and so on. The trick is to match the right approach, at the right place, the right time, and with the right people.

Direct approach

The direct approach gets to the heart of the matter quickly. Form a simple question and say it. Details come later. Asking a direct question is a good way to get a direct answer. People who like to give long, well-thought out answers veer away from terse one word, yes/no replies no matter how you ask. It's how they're wired. You can't change them.

Example

- "Will you pick up some milk on your way home?"
- "How do I dial out on your phone?"
- "Whom do I see about a refund?"

Last minute add-on

You want fries with that? After you've already said "Yes" to one or more items, it's not a stretch to say "Yes" again. Quick thinkers use this impulse to their advantage, as do salespeople. Buy a pair of shoes; add in matching hosiery. Select a sofa; add an accent pillow. Get a dozen roses; add a greeting card. Your granted request might have an easy accompaniment, an add-on you can get just by asking while the mood is favorable.

Example

"Will you iron my shirt? Thanks. And while you're at it, can you touch up my slacks?"

Bit by bit

Asking bit by bit is a way to get more over a longer period of time. For those with tight cash flow it's a way to portion out a purchase without having to rely on credit. Also, if your request sounds too large to ask all at once, try breaking it up into smaller pieces until you get everything you want.

Bob wanted a new set of tools and a roll-around cabinet to put them in. He figured that asking to buy everything at once would elicit objections from his wife. Instead, he explained his need to replace a few older tools and asked if there was anything she needed. He started by purchasing missing drill bits and socket wrenches. Later he told his wife he realized he needed a few more items and did she mind if he got a new drill with a battery pack? Later, he added a circular saw and a new miter box, which he used to complete a household project. He hung up his tools where he could and laid the rest out on the garage counter where they took up a lot of room. Finally, he went for the last item. He reasoned the tools deserved proper care and a roll-around cabinet should hold everything they had. The process took months, but Bob got his wish.

The whole enchilada

There are times when you need to ask for everything you want all at once. Keep in mind big requests need balance (fairness WIFM). The other person may need time to understand your needs. Pressing for an immediate answer could create resentment. Be realistic when there is much to consider, including the problems inherent when time constraints enter the picture. Have an idea of what you will give in return.

Example

"I've been thinking about our future and what I want out of life. I can't let go of this idea of going to nursing school. Nurses are always in demand. We could move anywhere and I'd be able to find a job. The only way it's going to happen is if I quit my job and concentrate on my studies from start to finish. We can get loans or even use part of the equity in our house. My grandmother said she'd help out. It would also mean you staying with your job. I know it's asking a lot. Will you work with me on this?"

Ask for more to get less

Ask for a new set of golf clubs and settle for that new titanium driver you have your eye on. That's the beauty of purposefully asking for more than you want. It's a lot easier to negotiate downward by giving up something of value and settling in where you hoped to be in the first place. You never know, you might get more than you thought.

Example

Your favorite music group is coming to town. The best tickets are sixty bucks each, too steep for your wallet, but the theater has good acoustics and the sound will be good even in the back row. You ask your spouse if she's interested and tell her about the sixty-dollar tickets. As predicted, she balks at spending over one hundred dollars for a pair of tickets. You acknowledge her concern and suggest seats costing twenty-five bucks per ticket. Suddenly, it's doable and you've got a date for the concert.

Sex sells

Unless you've been living in a cave, you know sex sells. It's one of the physical WIFM motivations. Do people use sex as a means to an end? Of course they do! They tantalize and seduce the other person to get what they want, which could be sex, a new article of clothing, or anything else. Men use it. Women use it. Be sure this is what you want before you use it. And even when going all the way isn't on the menu, a revealing neckline or a simple hug might be enough to subtly entice another to give you what you want.

Example

- "Is it okay if I buy those designer shoes I showed you in the magazine? I'll wear them in bed for you!"

- "Come on, it's just one dinner with my folks. What if I promise to make it worth your while after we come home?"

Flattery will get you somewhere

Sincere compliments are always appreciated. You are catering to another person's WIFM when you say something nice. When you know your audience, you know who likes to have it layered on a little thick. Phony compliments are the same thing as kissing up. Most folks don't care for that sort of thing, but some do, and others can't tell the difference. This may not be your favorite way to get what you want, but it's another form of give to get.

Example

- "How about wearing that outfit I gave you? You look so hot in it."
- "Will you go with me to the county fair? You make everything more fun!"
- "Can you help Junior with his homework? You know how to make history so much more interesting than I do."

Bold and beautiful

An unexpected bold statement can snap a person's head around. This is a direct approach with *Pow!* Want to get someone's attention? Come up with a doozy of a request and they're all ears. The topic has to be something unpredictable to bring about the desired shock or surprise, which could render their objections temporarily mute.

Example

- "I'm going to Peru next month. Want to come?"
- "I've decided to get a boob job. What do you think, should I go up two or three sizes?"
- "Are you ready to get me a sports car? Because I've picked one out."

Practice

Select one of these ways of asking that is outside your comfort zone. Over the next few days, try working it in to the way you ask for something.

More Ways to Ask

First you get someone's attention. Then you hold their interest by appealing to one or more of their WIFM motivations. This is different for everyone, but happily, there are lots of ways to reach out and ask for what you want.

Pick one

Choices are good. Give someone a choice that speaks to their WIFM and you have a better chance they'll pick one of the specific things you offer. Know what you want, state only the options you want, and let them choose. Will it be this or that?

Example

"Which appointment works better – 10am or 2pm?"

This is much different than asking, "Do you want to make an appointment?" That's a yes/no question that might not get you what you want. The open-ended question, "When do you want to get together?" is vague. It doesn't help pin down the specific time you prefer.

Judith's dad was not a control freak, but he did have a way of communicating with his kids so he got exactly what he wanted. He gave them choices – three to be exact – and each choice was something he wanted. He didn't ask the kids where they wanted to go on the weekend; he told them he would take them to one of three places – all places he wanted to go, and they could make the choice. Judith's dad was smart. He created a win-win situation.

Ha-ha!

Laughter is a universal language. In seconds it cuts through barriers that might otherwise take weeks of serious negotiations. Folks in a good mood are more obliging when it comes to giving you what you want. Be happy, show joy. Prompt the other person to laugh and you've taken a huge step forward. You've both let your guard down.

Though jokes are a setup, they're fun and can be used to break the ice. Spontaneous humor creates a shift that brightens the atmosphere. Laughter bonds because each person experiences the same positive, uplifting feeling. It levels the playing field and helps you out.

You can't force humor because then it isn't funny. It's best to try light humor with someone you don't know well until you gauge their response. Use laughter to segue to your request or use humor in your request. Too much joking around may give the impression you aren't serious about your objective. And in these times of political correctness, it's easy to cross the line into forbidden territory with humor once considered acceptable.

Example

- "Would you like to have dinner at my place? I picked up a juicy steak and a new fire extinguisher."

- (After a light moment.) "Too funny! I can see we're going to have a good time working together. Are you ready to take a look at this proposal?"

- "What do you say we replace this old wood deck with that new plastic lumber? It'll give the termites a new challenge."

Magnify your message

Showing emotion is an effective tool for persuading others. Your depth of emotion informs listeners about the importance or tone of your request, which in turn can make a difference in whether you get what you want.

Sounding dispassionate can put your respondent to sleep. It's amazing how many people barely open their mouths when they speak. Mumbling or lazy-sounding speech is hard to understand, it does not project confidence and works contrary to your aims. Modulate your voice to add interest. Add oomph! Your serious tone conveys the seriousness of the situation and your excitement transmits excitement. Choose words that magnify your message.

Example

"Honey, they only had one puppy left and it was the cutest thing you ever saw in your whole life! The little guy jumped into my lap and showered me with kisses. It was like we were already best friends. I asked the man to hold him for us until we could talk. I just know you're going to love him too! Want to come with me now and take a look?"

Dramatic presence

Those in dire straits are known to plead or beg. Your serious tone should match the peril of the situation. Be sure it does and you will be taken seriously.

An over-the-top performance for an underwhelming situation will be interpreted as theatrics, in which case you and your request could be dismissed. Teen-agers who engage in this type of drama get eye rolls from their parents. When it continues into adulthood, they get labeled "drama queens." When everything is a drama, nothing is.

Example

"Please, will you give me another chance? I made a mistake and I want to make it right. I'm dying inside. I'll do anything! Please?"

Squeaky wheel

Ah, the old squeaky wheel. There are times when you need to have your voice heard, not just once, but as many times as it takes to get what you want or need. Being the squeaky wheel gets annoying, so be careful you don't push too far or use it too often or you'll get tuned out.

The squeaky wheel is a form of persistence. You repeat your specific desire until it is met or you run out of steam and move on. The trouble behind being a squeaky wheel is in not identifying why your request has been ignored. Perhaps you are asking the wrong person or your request may not be high on their list. Ask yourself what has changed that would make the other person respond to you favorably the next time you ask.

Example

"Our dryer is broken again. It's doing that thing where it takes forever just to get warm. Can we get a new one?" (One week later.) "Your shirt? It's hanging on the line. It would be with the finished ironing if the dryer was working. Can we look for a new dryer?" (One week later.) "I spoke to a repairman today about our ten-year-old, unreliable dryer. He says it's going to cost almost as much to fix as it will be to buy a new one. If you don't have time tonight, we could go Saturday. Do you want to help pick one out?"

Semantics

A simple change in how you ask for something can be the determining factor in getting what you want. You might not think one word could make a huge difference. It can.

Suzie wanted to get her ears pierced. Her mom told her to wait until she was older. Suzie, using the squeaky wheel approach, asked the same thing over and over: "Can I get my ears pierced?" The answer was always "No." In desperation, Suzie asked her older sister for advice. The next time Suzie approached her mom, she changed her request to: "When can I get my ears pierced?" Suzie's mom saw the humor in the slight change and took her daughter to get her ears pierced. The change from "can I" to "when can I" added an assumption to the request that did the trick.

Be inventive

A stock question to a salesperson will likely yield a stock answer. Be inventive and find a new way to make your request. A good question makes the other person stop and think rather than respond by rote to the question they've heard a thousand times before.

Example

Change your request to your saleswoman from: "Can you show me your evening dresses?" to "Can you help me pick out a dress that tells my date 'I'm a fascinating woman with style?'"

Sugar-coated sandwich

It's not easy to tell folks what they don't want to hear. Like a bitter pill, it's easier to swallow with a little sugar wrapped around it. When you have a tough request, try sandwiching the front and back with words that are easier to take, like a compliment or incentive.

Example

"You've been a great neighbor. It's been very pleasant living next door to you all these years. But now that your kids are older, their language has gotten very coarse. They yell at each other in the street, honk their car horns and act up when you're not around. I've asked them to turn down their music and now I'm asking you to get a better grip on the situation. Can you do that? I sure would appreciate it. I want to keep things friendly."

Speak softly

Requests of a private nature may be best communicated in a whisper. Speaking softly so only one person can hear tells the other person your request is for their ears only. Being singled out makes them feel special and appeals to their emotional WIFM. This action implies intimacy and prompts the other to lean in close to hear every word of your private message.

Example

"Psst! Hey, Sis, come here! Listen: Mom and Dad dropped a hint that they want us to throw a surprise party at the club for their anniversary, but we're thinking about taking them on a three-day cruise instead. The pastor said he'd come along so they can renew their vows. Want to join in on this?"

The bigger, the better

Imagine the biggest, loudest way you could state your request. It could be on a billboard along a busy freeway, or a huge banner pulled by an airplane. It could be announced over the loudspeaker at a ballgame or posted on the giant scoreboard. Your request could be sung by a barbershop quartet or proposed over the radio. You could fill the horizon with skywriting or publish an ad in the newspaper.

Ask yourself whom you are trying to reach. Everyone you possibly can? One person? One person, but you want the world to know? Think of the giant impact your giant message could deliver. The possibilities are ginormous!

Etiquette and eloquence

There's beauty to the spoken word. It paints a picture, creates a mood and has the ability to impress with sophistication and style. Not everyone appreciates a good turn of phrase, but for those who do, a well-crafted request may earn you enough points to get what you want.

Saying "please" is not a lost form of communication. Kids are still taught to say the magic word before they can get what they want. Being an adult doesn't eliminate your need to say it. For added affect combine it with an eloquent request. Folks respond to being asked nicely. If you have to scream "Please!" the meaning has changed.

Example

"May I please have the honor of taking you to dinner?"

Focus on the positive

Emphasize positives when giving strong reasons why someone should grant your request and anticipate a positive response. Your positive attitude is catching. Likewise, undermining or insulting others does not endear them to you. In most cases, creating a hostile atmosphere is not conducive to getting what you want. You want to unify, bring the other person to your side – not divide. Make an effort to stay welcoming and inclusive.

Example

Change: "How can people donate to our cause when they're having trouble paying their own bills?" to "How about we put our focus this month on non-cash donations and see if we can drum up support for our thrift shop?"

Before her vacation, Leticia arranged for an economy-size rental car in her destination city and planned to use an upgrade coupon to get a mid-size model. At the car rental counter, she presented her coupon and asked about the possibility of getting an SUV, which was what she really wanted. The customer service representative said she couldn't give her the equivalent of a second upgrade. She could get the mid-size with the coupon; that was all. Rather than press the issue, Leticia stood at the counter smiling. In moments the rep said she would see what she could do and Leticia got her SUV.

Practice

Choose someone you interact with on a regular basis and turn up the kindness meter. In the course of general conversation you will ask questions. Afterward, did this person respond differently to you? How did the change in behavior feel to you?

Indirect Ways to Ask

Coming on too strong can make another person put up barriers. While asking for what you want shouldn't include setting up hurdles or an obstacle course, you may find stepping around the issue gets you to your target quicker. Choose an indirect, softer approach when it would seem overbearing to use a direct question.

Hint, hint

Delicate matters may take on an offensive aspect when spilled boldly onto the table. Try speaking of the issue with gentle language. Questions handled more discreetly through hints give others an opportunity to also avoid harsh terms. Do this by asking for something related to what you want. Taking a short step back from your intent leaves you close enough to the subject to relay your question without coming across like a brass band.

Example

- "How about we put on romantic music and light a candle?"

- "Want to cuddle tonight?"

Some folks prefer to *ask* indirect questions like these to convey their desire to make love and others prefer to *hear* the request this way. Asking the wrong way could be a turn-off.

Test the water

You may want something and feel hesitant to come right out and ask because you are unsure of the other person's response. How your request will be received could be dependent upon the strength of their WIFM. It doesn't hurt to test the water before you dive in with the real question.

Example

Suppose you want to rip out the lawn and greenery in your front yard to save on maintenance and water. Your idea is to replace it with colored stones and drought tolerant plants. Your spouse has a large flower garden in the front yard and takes pride in the overall appearance. You could say, "I want to lower our water bill. What if we took out the flowers and bushes and put in a cactus garden instead?" This question tests the waters by partially addressing your thoughts. It gets her thinking about what your plans might include. Her answer will tell you whether it's okay to get a little closer with your next point: "What I'd really like is to redo the entire front. I wouldn't miss mowing the lawn and we wouldn't be the first neighbors to pull ours out. Look at this picture I found in your garden magazine. We could make something nice like this, couldn't we?"

Plant seeds

Before you make your request, you may find it beneficial to plant seeds, that is, suggest what you want without actually coming out and asking for something specific. Your seemingly stray queries will generate some form of feedback, and you can follow up later on after your seeds have had time to germinate. The difference in time gives you ample opportunity to let ideas grow before making your real request. In the meantime you can be non-committal while you gather information.

Example

Say you are considering having another child. Your comments/ questions might run along these lines. "I'm thinking about holding on to this playpen for a while longer." Or, "Now that we've got two kids, I think it's true what they say about it getting easier. Wouldn't you agree?" You can continue to plant seeds with your comments and queries in the following weeks and months as your own thoughts and feelings develop. Eventually, you will have enough information to proceed with a more direct question.

A softened request

Words like *might, probably, could, would,* and *maybe* add an element of doubt or flexibility. The non-committed meaning takes the sharp edge off a direct question.

Example

- "Do you think maybe a private school would help Billy?"

- "Would bamboo furniture look good in the sunroom?"

The non-request request

You can hint at what you want by suggesting the query is not really for the person to whom you are speaking, which is part of the truth. This type of request creates a grey area. Should there be any offense taken at your question or presumed assumption, you can affirm you were asking generally and didn't mean it to apply to the person with whom you are speaking.

Example

"Do you know anyone who can donate lightly used children's items to the women's shelter thrift store?"

Third-party approach

You may find yourself in a situation where direct communication is undesirable or impossible. In a legal situation, you may prefer your attorney to speak for you. In the play *Cyrano de Bergerac*, the silver-tongued hero courts a woman on behalf of a handsome, but word-challenged suitor. Everything works out well in the end for Cyrano, but alas, it's a fictionalized tale. Whenever you choose another person to communicate on your behalf, you lose a level of control. Be sure you have a solid understanding with the one speaking for you. Be wary of lingering trust issues on how your situation will be handled. There's no point in feeling insecure with your mouthpiece. You may as well take matters into your own hands.

In some circles, the third-party approach is the norm. Typically, in junior high or middle school a girl will not ask a boy directly if he likes her and vice versa. The query is made and delivered through a friend. The friend acts as a buffer by providing a layer of protection and an opportunity to hear a truthful answer.

Practice

Think of something you want and write down how you would ask for it using the above indirect approaches. Then practice your script until you feel comfortable saying it.

Influencing Outcomes

The more you know about another person, the better chance you will have to influence the outcome of your request. Influence, not control. The only person you have control of is yourself. What you can do is introduce influential elements that will sway another to respond favorably.

Control issues

When dealing with people fond of exerting control or with someone in a position of authority, try to determine their WIFM motivations before you ask. Address those motivations and you've set yourself up in a position to negotiate.

Simply put, if your spouse likes chocolate, add chocolate to your request. If it's shopping, work that in. If your boss likes to be the center of attention, your ticket to success is to wrap your request around his needs. Know-it-all parents? Try catering to their desire to call the shots while at the same time asking for what you want.

Example

- "Honey, want to come to the hardware store with me? We can stop off at the mall on the way back."

- "Hey, boss, I've been thinking about what you said about trying new things. I found a new supplier I'd like to try out. If it's okay with you, I'd like to present her products at the next sales meeting."

- "Dad? Missy has to do a report on the Vietnam War. Could you share your stories, you know, spend a little time talking with her about it? We have plans tonight and I'd be happy to drop her off at your place."

What a great idea!

The key to getting what you want could be leading the other person to believe your desire was their idea in the first place. You can accomplish this in five easy steps.

1. Know what you want.

2. Decide what you want to say.

3. Present your ideas to the decision-maker.

4. Encourage the idea you want to see happen by showing excitement and adding in details.

5. Compliment the decision-maker on their great idea and emphasize you'll get on it right away.

Whitney worked at a publishing company as a production supervisor. It was her job to design and execute a monthly magazine cover. The editor, however, had the final say on the cover design. If he didn't like any of her ideas, it was back to the drawing board.

To get the cover she wanted, Whitney created three designs. In her opinion one was superior. The second was also very good, and the third was usually an off-beat alternative. She knew ahead of time which one she wanted (step one). She planned what she would say during the presentation (step two). She presented the designs and said a few words about each, using favorable words to describe the better choices and mentioning potential problems with the others (step three). At the first hint of a frown from the editor, she would pull away the weakest choice while suggesting why the first option had more going for it (step four). As the discussion continued, Whitney let the editor take the lead and agreed with his positive assessment of the best choice, confirming his decision by placing it on top of the pile and ending the meeting (step five). By following the five steps, Whitney ensured her portfolio of magazine covers was top notch.

Controlling control freaks

When you have a close relationship with someone you think is a control freak, chances are you know how they operate. Their personality provides a certain predictability you can use to your advantage. By anticipating the reaction of this person, you can plan ahead by coming up with a few likely scenarios where you can cater to this person without being patronizing, which in turn should help you get what you want. A few ways you can do this are:

- Give the person a task in which they can take total control while you handle other details.

- Exercise pacing to reduce their underlying anxiety.

- Suggest an activity, such as going to the movies, and let them pick the movie from a few you'd like to see.

- Find areas of agreement.

Control freaks generally have a lot of anxiety that they try to keep under control through rigid or controlling behavior. Your best bet is to make your request so it fits with this issue in mind.

You cannot really control control freaks any more than you can control anyone's behavior. People change when they are ready and want to change, and then it is a slow process. You don't change them. You are only responsible for your own behavior, so when you are forced to work with a control freak with authority, you might ask yourself if acceptance isn't the better option until you can make a better work arrangement.

Your influence makes a difference

While you can't fully control outcomes, you can influence others by playing to their motivations. Stay focused on what is within your realm and how others must play their part. Get your ducks in a row first by creating a plan, then go into action. In this way you increase your chances for success.

> *Christine wanted to remodel her kitchen. She was pretty sure her husband would say "No," but she decided to research what it would take to get it done. She thought of what he might object to: the cost, the mess, the inconvenience. After she had gathered her information and felt prepared to counter the objections he would surely raise, she waited for the right moment to ask her husband. When she laid out her ideas and plans, he surprised her by not raising any objections at all.*

Put the "go" in ego

When it comes down to it, does it really matter who comes up with the best idea? Be open to alternatives. Someone else's ideas could be better than what you had in mind. Being clever doesn't have to be a solo act. Call on the resources of others and leave your ego at the doorstep. Their point of view could reflect how they hope to help you. The possibility exists their solutions are to your advantage.

Practice

Think of an authority figure in your life or someone who likes to take control of situations. Imagine you need something from this person. Write down a few of their WIFM motivations. How might you integrate their desire to control outcomes with your request?

Negotiating Basics: Give to Get

Negotiating is about determining what is fair. For the many who believe they negotiate well – good for you! This chapter will help you strengthen your skills. If you shy away because you lack confidence in your negotiating abilities, remember, you are involved in simple, successful negotiations every day. Negotiations aren't only for purchase contracts. They include communications with family and friends in such a way that you don't give it a second thought.

Is it fair for you?

Negotiating is a fancy way of saying, "You give a little, you get a little." At its core is the fairness WIFM. Each of you has a balance scale that helps you determine what's fair, that is, how much you'll give versus how much you expect to get in return. Because you are all different and don't naturally agree on everything, you negotiate to find that balance. What you believe constitutes a fair trade may not match another's assessment. This is normal. Give yourself permission to enter into agreements that make sense for you.

Mutual cooperation allows the exchange to happen. In a negotiated retail transaction, you will be expected to part with your money in exchange for goods or services. When bartering, you exchange your goods or services for the other person's goods or services. Relationships require exchange on a multitude of levels and involve greater emotion.

Example

You:	"Hey, Adam, I need a logo design. Mindy said you're good at that. Do you think you could help me one evening this week?"
Adam:	"It depends on how complicated a design you want."
You:	"Nothing real fancy. A two-color graphic would work – like an outline of a surfboard and a wave, something that goes with surfing lessons to put on my business cards. I bet it will take you less than an hour. I'll pay you. How much do you want?"
Adam:	"When I did Mindy's logo she cooked dinner for me."
You:	"Believe me, you don't want me in the kitchen, but I could give you a surfing lesson."
Adam:	"That's cool. I've never gone surfing. Can you come Wednesday after work?"
You:	"Sure. Is six-thirty okay?"
Adam:	"Yeah. Come to my apartment. We can set a time for the lesson later on."

Say What?

Good communication is integral to good negotiations and good relationships. You communicate your side; the other party listens. You told them, but did they get it? You are responsible for your part of the communication and that includes making sure the other person understood your request. The listener is not only hearing your side, but is responsible for confirming their understanding. This back and forth volley continues until your conversation is over. At the end, did you both get it?

To be responsible for both giving your message and receiving theirs requires mental presence. You've got a head full of ideas, desires, catchy songs, to-do lists, and past conversations fighting for your attention. You will need to focus when both speaking and listening. Choose words that clearly convey your meaning. Give your full attention when it's your turn to listen.

How do you know for sure whether others comprehend the conversation? It's okay to ask if they're following along and even suggest they repeat to you their understanding. Otherwise, you assume they understand, and you might be wrong. When listening, it's up to you to make sure you understand. You can say, "If I hear you correctly, you're telling me that ..." This confirmation will increase comprehension and allow for smoother negotiations.

Basing your interaction on assumptions, or guessing at what the other person means will increase the likelihood of misunderstandings, which in turn may lead to conflict. Other people don't think, act or feel exactly as you, and to assume they would or should is not a basis for a solution or effective communication. Do not leave lingering questions about your agreement to chance. Put everything in writing to remove all doubt.

Rather than drive her kids to and from school every day, Mia decided it would be beneficial to offer a simple exchange of services with Sean, the father of her daughter's friend, to carpool every other week. They agreed to take turns so each would drive one week and be off the next. It was an uncomplicated negotiation that resulted in fair treatment for both parties and also allowed Mia to set up a work schedule weeks in advance because she could plan around her obligation. The arrangement worked fine until the kids had a one week vacation at Thanksgiving, Mia's normal drive week. Sean felt it was unfair for Mia to have an extra week off from driving and wanted her to resume when the kids' vacation ended. Mia's work schedule was already set, but that didn't matter to Sean. Mia and Sean could no longer get what they needed from one another and their arrangement came to an abrupt halt. After scrambling for a replacement, Mia ended up driving her kids to school every morning and found someone else to take them home.

This story serves as a reminder of how day-to-day interactions involve negotiations and why you probably have more experience than you recognize. A negotiation is successful when both parties feel the value received is equal to the value given – or better still, when both parties feel they got the better end of the bargain.

Mia's story also illustrates that circumstances can change and a negotiated deal can fall apart. Stay flexible with options and be open to renegotiate. People change and so do WIFM motivations. When you find out which motivations have greater bearing, you can decide if you are prepared to meet the other person's new expectations or requirements and vice versa.

Mia and Sean started out with an equal trade of services. If both parties were amenable, Sean could have continued to drive all the kids both ways every day and Mia could have asked to barter another service such as babysitting on the weekend or running errands. She could have given Sean gas money, offered to cook a gourmet meal once a week, or taken all the kids to an amusement park or museum once a month as long as their agreement was in effect.

Be creative in your thinking and you will discover solutions. When you aren't sure what your negotiating points are, that is, what value you have to give, start a discussion with the other person and ask what's important to them. Inquire about unmet needs in seemingly unrelated areas. For example, if Sean liked Mia's babysitting proposal, he and his wife could plan a date night. Or, if he accrued many hours, Mia could take the kids for a weekend so he and his wife could get away for a mini-vacation.

Value is subjective and must be established. When the services, material goods, public relations or goodwill you offer hold no value for the other person, you will receive nothing in return. Your negotiation will falter until you find the appropriate value in the eyes of the other person.

Get a head start

It can be to your benefit to jump the gun and give value first, before negotiations begin. Whatever you give or do for the other person, you will get a head start by tipping the scales to your advantage. Giving value first is a sign of good faith. It puts you in a position similar to a benefactor. Others tend to see you in a favorable light. However, when you give first, do so *without specific expectation*. Enjoy the feeling you get by giving first and giving freely. You cannot give freely and at the same time expect something in return from another, even though you may receive something later. Unmet expectations of reciprocity lead to disappointment and resentment.

Hidden value in negotiations

Give and take in personal relationships may not involve goods or services. It is likely your negotiations will involve emotions. The value you give and receive comes from feelings, beliefs and other intangibles.

Example

- You give your friend a haircut because it's an enjoyable way for you to express your creativity, not because he's willing to buy you dinner.

- You ask your spouse to read to you at bedtime because not only does she correctly pronounce words you don't know well, it also brings you closer together and generates warm feelings for your spouse.

- You agree to drive your young niece to her violin recital because you love and support her. In turn she's agreed to spend the rest of the day with you for cookie baking fun.

Acknowledge your past negotiating successes however small, and then expand your current knowledge to new situations. Lack of confidence negotiating in a particular situation can be overcome through gaining knowledge, allowing for flexibility, practice, or could even include the help of another with more experience. Ask for help from someone you trust.

Practice

The next time you want to ask for something, first consider what you have of value to contribute to the negotiation. Decide whether what you have to give is equal to what you hope to receive. Should your offer prove weak from the other's point of view, create a back-up plan for finding options that will better match the other person's WIFM.

Bargaining and Bartering

Bargaining and bartering are both forms of negotiation. Bargaining generally includes negotiating for goods or services for less than the asking price. Barter is about trading goods or services for other goods or services without exchanging cash. In both instances, you have an opportunity to get what you want. Just ask!

Everyone likes a bargain

Everyone likes a bargain, but not everyone likes to bargain. Lots of folks think bargaining for a better deal is limited to cars and houses. Some of you feel the stated price of a given item is there for good reason, one you don't care to question. In some cultures, folks are offended when others try to haggle during yard sales. You may think bargaining is looked down upon or something to be avoided, yet you have no idea how many others anticipate you will offer them something other than the stated price. They've even built that expectation into the price. You don't ask; they get extra profit, a bonus offset by the times when they give more for less.

Bargaining for a lower price is a frequent request, though you may be more interested in receiving another kind of value such as a warranty, extra accessory or specific service thrown in. How do you bargain? You come right out and ask!

Suppose you are at a garage sale and see a few items you like including a lawn mower tagged at fifteen dollars. You have many angles from which to choose how to ask for a better price. Have an idea of what you think is an acceptable deal before you begin.

Example

- "Would you take ten dollars for that lawn mower?"
- "If I buy your lawn mower, will you throw in that four-dollar red gas can for free?"
- "Can you give me a special price on the mower if I buy a bunch of your gardening tools?"
- "How badly do you want to sell that lawn mower?"

The seller may accept your offer without hesitation. If she makes a counter-offer or sticks with her original price, you have the option of accepting the counter or coming up with your own counter-offer. Here's what you can say next.

- "Will you take twelve dollars for the mower?"
- "Is it okay if I buy the mower for fifteen and give you two bucks for the gas can?"
- "How many tools would I have to buy to get a better discount?"
- "If I come back in a couple of hours and the mower is still here, will you sell it to me for ten bucks?"

Bargaining can be fun, but it's not a game. Find agreement and then be sure to follow through with your end of the deal. Otherwise you're just wasting the other person's time.

How hard you bargain is up to you. Hearing the word "No" is not a big deal to some folks and won't keep them from asking a second or third time. Persistence pays. Being annoying is a drag. A change in body language or tone of voice will tell you the other person's level of annoyance. You still have choices. You can stay firm, back away with a softened offer, or get tough and risk further ire. Persisting with demands when the other person is annoyed is a sure way to bring out their stubborn nature.

Mall kiosks, farmer's markets, swap meets and garage sales are good locations to try out your new bargaining skills. Asking the owner or other decision-maker for a discount can cut corners. Salespeople are frequently empowered to offer a set discount without calling in a manager or owner. You could find that amount – just ask.

Consignment shops are great for bargains. In some stores the price of the merchandise drops after sitting for thirty days. After sixty days, the price drops again. The shop owner may have an arrangement with the consignees to discount a certain percentage without calling for permission, which means you can bargain right on the spot. Ask if you can get a lower price than the one marked.

After hearing about a cosmetic cream for problem skin and watching a video at a mall kiosk, Cindy decided to buy the product. It was $60.00 a jar, more than she was prepared to spend. The saleswoman offered a free gift with purchase. Cindy had no use for the gift and therefore it held no value. She wanted a hefty discount. The saleswoman offered a small amount off the price and Cindy declined. After some hesitation, the salesperson then offered to do something special for Cindy by extending her own employee discount. Cindy didn't believe the saleswoman's explanation, but she also didn't care. She wanted the product at the lower price and the sale was made.

Most folks don't know they can bargain at larger retail stores for goods or services. A store with dozens or even hundreds of locations has to make money on every sale. A small profit adds up when you work in high volume. You'd be amazed at what you can get when you ask.

Burt went into a major chain department store looking for $90.00 shoes he'd seen on sale for $45.00. He asked the salesman to bring out a pair in both black and brown. The advertised shoe Burt wanted was not available in his size and the salesman brought out a similar style in both colors. Burt liked the alternate style, but unfortunately they were $75.00 each and not on sale. He told the salesman he wanted the shoes, but he would not pay retail. Furthermore, he said it was not his fault the store had run out of his size and if they wanted to make a sale he would be willing to pay the $45.00 sale price. The salesman could not accept Burt's offer, but scurried off and returned with a coupon he could scan for a $20.00 discount. Burt decided to take both pair of shoes and paid $55.00 each.

Bartering

Money isn't the only means of exchange, and when economic resources are in short supply you are wise to think outside the box. You need cash to pay your mortgage and cable TV bill, but you have other items and services of value you can use to barter for other goods and services.

Renewed popularity in barter means numerous web sites exist where you can find someone who not only has what you want, but wants what you have. You could post your own wants along with what you have to trade and someone could find you. You can even make a three-way trade. Word-of-mouth and networking are great ways to spread the word. Let others know what you're looking for every time you speak with someone new. Pick up the phone, use e-mail and social networking sites, or post a notice on a community bulletin board.

Let's make a deal!

How do you approach someone you don't know, such as a tradesman, about trading services? You ask your extended network for a recommendation, look for newspaper ads, or do an Internet search. Then you contact the tradesperson. You could say something like, "Hi, I got your name from so-and-so. I need new tile installed in my hall bathroom and I'm trying to find someone who will trade services with me. I do alterations and mending. And I also make custom quilts in any size. Would you be interested in working out a trade?" Your trade could involve part cash, part services.

Barter options range from simple to exceedingly complex transactions. In any case, you need confidence the other person will make good on their side of the agreement. Overcoming trust issues is easier with people you know, but that doesn't mean you don't have to be crystal clear about your arrangement. You can write out your arrangement and both of you can sign it.

When dealing with strangers, be sure to check appropriate resources: up-to-date licenses, bonds, workman's comp. insurance, recent complaints, and so on. Be prepared to provide the same. You may not be exchanging money, but your trade involves value, which is why what you receive could be considered reportable income.

Ask yourself what you want and what you have to offer. Are you an accountant in need of plumbing? An English tutor in need of disc brakes? I'm aware of arrangements involving: an artist who received dental work in exchange for a couple of paintings, a masseuse and a hair stylist trading services, and a graphics company that created a brochure in exchange for a dozen strawberry cheesecakes. It doesn't matter how outlandish your request sounds. All that matters is the parties come to an agreement. But first, you have to ask.

Practice

Brainstorm with a friend or write out the various services you have to offer in lieu of cash. Next, take an inventory of items you have around your house or in storage that would be of value to another. These are the goods and services you have to offer. Now what is it you need? Put these together and you have the potential to get what you want while giving someone else something of value.

Reactive and Proactive Approaches to Overcome Objections

You thought your request was reasonable and yet it was denied. Why? You missed the other person's WIFM motivations or didn't accurately assess how much weight they would carry. Anytime you ask for anything, it's normal for objections to arise. People want more information or a reason why they should grant your request. They throw in a roadblock or two. Break away those blocks and you've moved farther down the road toward success.

Planning ahead means anticipating objections and knowing how to overcome them. Here are two choices. One is to be reactive and deal with each objection as it comes up. The other is to be proactive by removing the objection before you make your request. You may end up with a combination of these two.

Reactive response

By waiting for objections, you put yourself in a potentially defensive position. You ask your question. They toss back a problem. You suggest a resolution. They ask for more information. You provide information and they toss over another objection. The conversation volleys back and forth until all objections are resolved or you reach a stalemate. Each objection fits in with the other person's WIFM. On the positive side, you could make a request and the other person might grant it with no further discussion.

Example

You: "I'm thinking about inviting the guys over for Sunday's game. You didn't make any plans, did you?"

Spouse: "Do you mean you want me around to help cook and clean up? Because you know I couldn't care less about the game." (Objection.)

You: "You don't have to cook. We're going to pick up hot wings and stuff. I promise we won't leave a mess. Jackson wants to bring his new girlfriend and I thought you might like to hang out with her."

Spouse: "Is this the girlfriend with the four-year-old boy?" (Request for more information.)

You: "Yes."

Spouse: "Well, if she wants to go shopping, that would be okay." (Approval.)

You: "Great! I'll tell Jackson to bring them and I promise we'll clean up." (Reinforcement.)

Put the "pro" in proactive

By taking a proactive stance you present information and/or discuss subjects ahead of time, including topics that could elicit objections, and present solutions up front. This removes potential roadblocks before you make your actual request. Knowing your audience helps you anticipate what that particular person would find objectionable. Tell them what they want to hear and the objection is no longer an issue.

Example

You: "I'm thinking about inviting the guys over for Sunday's game. I told Jackson we should pick up some hot wings and stuff so we can clean up a little easier. We're not going to leave a mess like last time. He's got that new girlfriend, the one with the four-year-old boy. If you're not doing anything, do you want to go shopping with them while the guys and I watch the game?"

Spouse: "Yeah, that sounds good. Tell him to bring her over and then we'll go to the mall."

Being proactive doesn't mean the other person still won't have objections. You can't anticipate every objection imaginable or present everything up front. Requests for information may send you away until you can provide enough of what the other person needs for them to say "Yes." Or, you could get a hurdle too tall to overcome.

You can't always get what you want

As you know, you won't always get what you want. No matter how many objections you have to overcome, sometimes the answer will not go your way. Look to the other person's WIFM motivations for a better understanding of their position. Sometimes your best arguments are not sufficient to overcome their WIFM, even if they say it's because they have your best interest at heart. Ask what you could do for the other person that would make them change their mind.

Example

You: "I'm thinking about inviting the guys over for Sunday's game. Jackson is going to pick up some hot wings. I promise we'll clean up. Anyway, he's going to bring his girlfriend and her four-year-old son. Do you want to go shopping with her while we watch the game?"

Spouse: "I don't think so. We discussed this last time after you left me a big mess. You promised me you'd trade off with Jackson. He can have everyone over to his house."

You: "But we have a wide screen. The game looks so much better. We can go to his house next time."

Spouse: "No. Our agreement was every other time and it's Jackson's turn. You promised last time that you wouldn't leave a mess and you did. So, forget it. Tell Jackson you'll bring the hot wings. I'm staying home to finish my project before my Monday staff meeting."

Practice

The next time you'd like to ask for a favor, think of the other person's WIFM and what information they would want before they would say "Yes." Start a dialogue and include this information. During your conversation, listen carefully to what is being said. Think about what objections they might have and how you can solve those problems before making your request.

Tips to Overcome Objections

There are as many ways to overcome objections as there are ways to ask for what you want. Tricks and tips are helpful, but it all boils down to appealing to the WIFM of the person granting your request. Have you been able to give the other person enough of what they want in order for them to give you what you want? Here are a few more situations to help you understand how to get more of what you want.

As part of her duties at her local university women's club, Florence was tasked with finding scholarship money that would be awarded to high school girls interested in pursuing the sciences. Her group had not yet received their non-profit status and most of the companies contacted would only give ten or twenty dollars because they could not write off the donation. Florence owned stock in a small, local science/tech company and it occurred to her to write the company president about her cause. She asked for a donation large enough to send one or more teens to summer science camp, and cited the possibility the young women might one day contribute to that very same company. The company sent $700, enough to enable one lucky student to attend science camp that year.

Objections are meant to be overcome

Initial denials are objections to be overcome. When you hear "No," there is usually a reason that explains the objection. Ask for an explanation if none was provided. The reason, assuming it's truthful, will give you the WIFM motivation. Then you can work with it.

Example

Spouse: "No, you can't have any pumpkin bread."

You: "Why not?"

Spouse: "I'm taking it to the potluck."

You: "You're going to slice it, right? Couldn't you give me a sliver from the middle and then arrange it on the plate?"

Not everyone will want to give away their personal reasons for turning down your request. That's part of their WIFM and there may be nothing you can do to change it.

Example

Mom: "No."

You: "Can you please tell me why?"

Mom: "Because I said so."

Diffuse conflict with agreement

You are seeking agreement with your request and nothing diffuses conflict like finding common ground. It's important to acknowledge the other person's point of view even if it differs from your own. Nothing takes the wind out of the sails from an argument faster than to agree with what the other person said. To be convincing you must:

- Take responsibility for your actions
- Show honest compassion for the other's viewpoint
- Do not offer excuses

Example

Friend: "No. Last time I lent you money you didn't pay me back until two months later."

You: "That's true. I felt badly about not being able to keep that arrangement. You might remember it's not because I didn't want to pay you back. My car repair was more involved than they said it would be. I paid you as soon as I could. This time, I don't have anything in the way and I get paid Friday."

No buts about it

Let's say you make your request and you hear, "Yes, but…" This doesn't mean "Yes, we agree." However it is a sign you are on the right track. You're partially in agreement and there is still at least one objection to be overcome. After the word "but" you will hear the objection, hopefully the real one. Finding out the true objection isn't always easy, and hearing it is no guarantee the outcome will change.

Example

You: "Wasn't I supposed to get my security level upgrade today?"

Boss: "Yes, but you'll have to wait."

You: "How come?"

Boss: "I don't know; some software problem. It's on hold."

Yes, and...

When you are countering an objection, avoid saying "Yes, but…" For the reason stated above, the other person will hear why you still aren't in agreement. Instead, remove the word "but" from your end of the conversation and replace it with "and." Saying "Yes" states agreement. Use "and" to make a point separate from your agreement. You can use it to turn the disagreement around to your favor.

Example

You: "Would it be all right if I borrowed your car?"

Uncle: "No. The last time you didn't replace the gas you used."

You: "Yes, and that's why this time I'll be filling it up."

I'm right, you're wrong

Agreeing with another might seem like a monumental challenge when you both have different versions of the same event. No one wins when you insist you're right and they're wrong, or vice versa. Find agreement on small points and remember three things:

1. You can't make another person wrong.

2. Focus on identifying with their feelings.

3. Use "I" statements.

Example

You: "Will you go out with me?"

Friend: "How can you even think that when last time you stood me up?"

You: "I understand why you're angry. I would be angry, too, if I didn't think you even tried to get in touch. I did leave a message – twice. I believe you that you didn't get them. Can we put this behind us and try again?"

Watering it down

Not everything is about you, which means that when you hear "No" the possibility exists that someone else's reason has nothing to do with you. There are times when circumstances beyond your control, or those of the person you asked, are the deciding factors. In those cases, the objection doesn't matter. You can't get to the bottom of it to effect change.

It's a common assumption to think the reason you heard "No" is because you asked for too much. Until you know whether you are totally out of the equation, don't be in a hurry to water down your request. Your first impulse might be to ask for less in the mistaken notion that it will be easier for you to get some of what you want.

Example

Boss: "A four-percent raise isn't going to happen right now."

You: "Can I get two percent?"

Boss: "I'll get back to you."

When the "No" you get isn't about you, there's nothing to be gained by asking for less. You only serve to get yourself less later when it is about you. Don't water down; wait until you know why you were turned down. Circumstances could change allowing your original request to go through.

Example

Boss: "Great news, we've got a new budget and you'll be getting that two percent raise you wanted."

You: "What happened to four percent?"

Boss: "You seemed okay with two percent so I used that when figuring my budget."

Once you've watered down your request, you've made it very difficult to climb back up to where you want to be. Do yourself a favor and sit tight.

Walk away

Those of you who have visited a country where bargaining is the norm know that the strongest thing you can do is walk away during your negotiation. The shop owner, who scoffed at your offer, will suddenly come up with a counter-offer. He may even run after you with the item in hand. The last thing he wants is to be undersold by a neighboring vendor, and as soon as you show disinterest the price drops.

This technique is handy anywhere negotiations take place. It's been said that the first person to walk away wins, and the first person to cave to pressure loses. In my opinion there are no losers, as no deal happens unless both parties are reasonably satisfied. If you choose to walk away, be prepared to not look back.

Practice

When you get turned down on your request, pause for a moment of silence. Listen to your self-talk and hear what goes through your mind. Instead of reacting with the first thing that pops into your head, take a few seconds to consider your best move.

More Tips to Overcome Objections

Your objection tool belt is well-equipped with gadgets to handle most objections. Utilize them to help get what you want.

One tool is to be direct and ask plainly why your request was turned down. Phrase this as an open-ended question and allow the other person the freedom to say what is on their mind. Judgments or a harsh tone on your part give the other person a reason to withhold. This is a time to gather information and you want to create an atmosphere where the other person feels safe in giving their explanation. Be receptive to what is said.

Miscommunication is a missed opportunity

Hearing a "No" to something you want may trigger an urge to respond with emotion before you have heard an explanation. Your surprise or disappointment could be premature. Before you let loose with emotion, ask the person how he came to that conclusion. Let him talk without interruption. Be a good listener first before you form an opinion. Then, when you express your emotions, they will be based on the whole story.

Be open to what the other person is telling you. Repeat it back in your own words to be sure you understand. Resist the temptation to interpret what has been said to suit your own agenda. Miscommunication can lead to undesired results and lost opportunities. If you are unsure, ask for further clarification.

Example

HR: "I'm sorry, we're not hiring for that position now."

You: "Are you saying this is a temporary situation?"

HR: "No. That position has been eliminated and combined with Accounts Payable. You can apply for that job instead."

Second that emotion

After your turndown and an explanation from the other person, you may feel you didn't convey your emotions as strongly as you felt them. Might the other person have a change of heart if they knew what your request meant to you? This is possible when you share a strong emotional WIFM motivation. Asking the exact thing in a louder tone of voice offers nothing new. You need emotion, which is a voice from the heart plus facial and body expression. Offer new information to help strengthen your position and you cover even more WIFM territory.

Example

Spouse: "No, we won't have time for a side trip. And Krakow? We agreed to travel Germany. The kids are expecting us to take them to that castle that looks like Disneyland."

You: "The thing is I told my mom I'd visit the old village while she's still alive so I could tell her about it. After she fell last week, I got to thinking. I want her to know I haven't forgotten my promise. I think it's important, and the kids could learn about their heritage."

Hah! That's a good one

Humor is a great equalizer. Being funny opens doors as long as it's clear you are not making fun of another's objection. Not everyone can be witty with a quick retort, although spontaneity might accomplish your objective. Be silly or a little goofy to boost creativity. Throw in a little charm, laugh, show love or another endearing positive emotion to win over the other person.

Example

You: "Can you find a place to squeeze in this umbrella?"

Spouse: "Forget it. There's no room. The car is already overstuffed."

You: (Twirl the umbrella and imitate Charlie Chaplin's penguin walk.)

Spouse: "Ha! Okay. Slide it in behind the passenger seat."

The take away

If you've ever dieted, you know that as soon as you deprive yourself of dessert there's nothing you crave more than two chocolate cookies with a layer of ice-cream sandwiched inside. You want what you can't have. This same odd phenomenon can come up during negotiations. You offer something of value and it's ignored, that is, until you remove it from the table. Suddenly, the other person can't get enough of it. Don't be caught by surprise – use it for leverage.

Example

Suppose you bought a computer with all new accessories for your home office. Now you are negotiating to trade your old computer for your friend's unused art supplies. Your objective is to match the perceived value of your old computer equipment with the perceived value of her art supplies. Your friend has a keyboard, mouse and monitor in her current set up, but her computer has died, which is why she is interested in yours. Her lack of interest in the accessories is an objection. She is saying "No" to these items by her indifference.

You: "Since you don't seem interested in my old keyboard, mouse and monitor, I suppose I could sell them at a garage sale. Someone will want them."

Friend: "Wait a minute. I didn't say I wouldn't take them. Your old monitor is a little bigger than mine and I wouldn't mind having an extra mouse."

You: "Well, okay, if you want to include them, how about throwing in another blank canvas?"

A smaller objection

You may be closer to getting what you want than you realize. This is true when you already have partial agreement. Your goal is to get full agreement. The objection is the difference between the two, a much smaller portion to overcome.

Example

Suppose you and your spouse are willing to buy a new flat screen TV with a base price of $1,000.00, except you want the fancier, more expensive model at $1,275.00. Together you've agreed to spend $1,000.00, so you're part way there. Think of it this way: the question isn't about spending the full $1,275.00. Your challenge is to show the value of the difference, the extra $275.00 – a much smaller amount. You can do that, can't you? Or, you could be the one wanting the base model. Your challenge is to take away the extra TV features as not holding value to justify the price.

Practice

The next time you have partial agreement, focus your energy on the difference between what you have already agreed to and your final destination, and experience how this slants the focus of the subsequent conversation.

Get Tough and Pump It Up

Important matters can be stalled or ignored for only so long. You asked nicely. You went through the proper channels and tried your best to overcome objections. You filled a notepad with doodles while waiting on hold, sent e-mails, wrote a letter, called three more times and you're stuck in neutral. Now what? It's time to get tough and pump it up. Imagine how the solutions below could help you get action.

Did you reach the right person?

Asking the wrong people will get you nowhere, no matter how many times you try. Much like a call screener, your initial contact could be acting as a line of defense keeping you from reaching the proper person in authority. Find out. You could say something like, "You don't seem to be able to address this problem. Should I be talking to your boss?" Employees formerly unable to help suddenly remember a way to get you what you want without having to bother their boss. Other times, they are more than glad to pass you off to someone else, a move propelling you forward toward a chance of success.

Arlene is a no-nonsense woman who doesn't want to bother with low-level employees. She goes straight to the top with her requests, and has called several company presidents and CEOs. The trick, of course, is actually getting through to them. The CEO's secretary will screen her call by asking if he knows why Arlene is calling or if the CEO is expecting her call. Arlene replies, "He wouldn't want anyone else to know why I'm calling." This remark creates doubt in the secretary's mind. She can't ask Arlene anything further without potentially going against her boss and it sounds like Arlene's spoken to him before. A number of CEO's have taken Arlene's calls. Perhaps it's shock or her sense of humor, but once she gets through, CEO's help Arlene.

HEY, YOU!

Forget nice. Now you feel like yelling, but will it help your cause? Yelling can set you back. Those who are turned off by yelling may tell you to turn the volume back down or leave, causing you to lose your opportunity.

Those who yell relate to those who also yell, which means you will occasionally encounter individuals who won't understand the full extent of your needs until you project them at full volume. Be careful to stick to the subject and do not lose control. Name-calling is for five-year-olds and swearing is never proper. You'll only come across as foul-mouthed or unable to control your temper. Find the right words to state your case. Yelling to intimidate is bullying.

Assertive does not equal aggressive

Violence is not the answer to your question unless you're angling for a lawsuit or a jail cot. Don't make your situation worse by getting physical. An upset buyer in my auto finance office took a swing at his salesman and fortunately missed. Though the customer was not angry with me, I would not allow the man to return to my office. Arranging the completion of his contracts made the customer's life more difficult and at the conclusion he was banned from the dealership.

First do no harm

The expression: "Words said in haste are regretted in leisure" is an appropriate reminder to think before you speak. Make an effort to let off steam before charging in with an angry exchange. A slow count to ten can give you a needed pause. Or, breathe in to a count of three and exhale to a count of three. Use this short mental break to refocus your intent to stay on subject. Leave out foul language and speak slowly to communicate your message. Despite what your self-talk says, other people don't make you angry. The anger you feel comes from you. Own your feelings, no matter what they are, by speaking in "I" statements. To prevent "foot-in-mouth disease," ask for information without making an accusation.

Example

Change: "Are you telling me this to make me jealous?" to "Why are you telling me this?"

Clayton was mad because he had done some work for a man who didn't pay him. He was too angry to call and ask for the money. Instead, he sat down and crafted a vitriolic business letter. He showed the letter to his friend, Jane, who happened to stop by Clayton's office. She encouraged him to put all his anger into the letter and hold nothing back. After a few drafts she told him the letter was complete and now he should tear it up. Clayton was livid. He had put great emotion into the letter and spent a lot of time on it. Jane explained the exercise was to put the anger where it wouldn't do harm – in an unsent letter. Clayton directed the last of his negativity into tearing up the letter. He took a deep breath and called his errant customer. Clayton was able to channel his anger into a more appropriate stern business voice. The two were able to work out a payment plan.

Pump up the emotion

As you know, heartfelt emotions help get your point across. An impassioned plea is known to melt a heart of steel. Compassionate listeners respond to emotion and a few genuine tears express more than facts. If you feel the tears coming on, let them out! Don't use crying as a ploy, and don't fake it. You'll annoy the other person and once they roll their eyes, you've lost credibility.

People who nag and whine do not project confidence, they annoy. Repetition has its place. However its frequent use labels you a nag. Find a better way to communicate before you earn this moniker. Whining is the opposite of pumping it up. Use your voice and emotion to put some *oomph* behind your request.

Unhappy customers are within their rights to be stern. Stating your concern in a no-nonsense tone conveys your serious desire to find a remedy.

> *Evelyn called a heating/air-conditioning repair company to troubleshoot the problem with her faulty air conditioning. The company sent a fellow who played around with the thermostat and claimed the problem could be fixed with an expensive repair. As a watchful senior, Evelyn was skeptical. From what she could tell, the only thing the repairman had done was mess with her thermostat setting. By phone, she let the company know she felt scammed. After some back and forth, Evelyn asked the company what they would do for her. They sent out their best guy who did a thorough cleaning of the system, both inside and out, fixed the problem, and offered her two years of free maintenance, more than she expected.*

That's a laugh

Outrageous humor and unconventional acts orchestrated for surprise take ingenuity to concoct, but nothing opens another person like a good laugh. You are more likely to win people over to your side when they feel good and feel good about you. Practical jokers pull stunts for effect and radio disc jockeys get press for crossing the line. Do you have the nerve to dress up as a cow and carry a protest sign stating your intent to "mooove" your business elsewhere?

Extra! Extra!

Plan a protest and bring in the press. Let the problem company know of your plans. Your picket may translate into a loss of business and negative PR. They may be more interested in solving your issues than speaking to a reporter or losing revenue. The bottom line is a financial WIFM. Hit them where it hurts. Know your rights and stay within the law.

Television stations and newspapers frequently employ a trouble-shooter to take on a cause for the little guy. Stop asking yourself why the offending party doesn't return your phone calls and turn your troubles into a human-interest story. Let someone else help you get results. Call your local station or other media outlet and ask how to submit your problem.

Call in the reinforcements

Another way to be heard is a letter writing campaign. Internet missives have taken the place of post cards and are a quick way to gather steam and strength in numbers. Social networking can get your message to literally millions of readers. Rally others behind your cause and let viral marketing do the rest. It's a proven way to get things done.

Government offices can give you the name of an ombudsman to help with specific problems. Check your local Internet government pages to see what's available. There may be a department where you can lodge a complaint, be guided toward a designated mediator or enlist legal action.

And, speaking of legal action, how many of you have ever written a letter threatening to turn the matter over to your attorney, even when you didn't have one? There's nothing wrong with saying you're considering legal action if your matter is not settled satisfactorily within a certain period of time. Whether you choose to actually hire an attorney is up to you. The response you get depends on the other person's WIFM and the strength of your case. Companies have been known to settle without admitting wrongdoing to keep costs down, keep their PR up and get rid of you. On the other hand, if you ask your renters to move out and they don't because their WIFM means free rent for as long as they can stay on your property, you may have to hire someone to serve papers and eventually get them evicted.

Ask for help

Do you know anyone else who may hold sway or intercede on your behalf? A clergyperson, professional, or known third party has the advantage of implied impartiality. Network. Ask your friends, family or co-workers for the name of someone who would go to bat for you or otherwise help your cause.

How far will you go to get what you want? You can hire professional counsel, whether legal, medical, therapeutic or otherwise. Listen to it and get a second opinion if needed. In a legal matter when the courts rule against you, and your loved ones are telling you to drop it, your WIFM for vindication may be stronger than the merits of your case. Do you appeal to a higher court or do you move on? Only you know the answer to this one.

Ultimatums

You want…or else! An ultimatum might be chosen after more civil methods have been tried with no success. It's a get tough approach that utilizes your power to effect change by striking at the core of deeply felt WIFM motivations. Your words will convey desperation and finality, a "my way or the highway" proposition. Be prepared to follow through. Only you know how important getting your request is and what you'll do to get it.

Example

- "Either you go to AA starting tonight or else I'm calling your boss on Monday and telling her you need their Employee Assistance Program. What'll it be?"

- "You have two months to either start college, or get a job and start paying rent. Otherwise, I'm throwing your mattress on the curb and turning your bedroom into my craft room. Which is it?"

Others don't like to be forced into a position where they feel intimidated by psychological and/or emotional manipulation. What seems like "tough love" to you might feel like bullying to another. Your justification of the matter could have you believe you were forced to make the ultimatum. Ultimatums do not have to involve physical, emotional or mental distress, or in any way be abusive. A terse statement of fact can suffice. Be responsible for your actions. Issuing ultimatums comes at a cost. You can expect consequences whether or not your request is granted.

Once threats or promises have left your mouth, you may have second thoughts and decide to back off. Don't let foolish pride or stubbornness stand in the way of a reasoned decision. New possibilities could arise allowing for reconsideration.

Practice

Stand in front of a mirror and ask for something like you mean it. Look at your body language and listen to the tone of your voice. What would your reaction be if you were on the other side of the mirror? Make adjustments to your delivery until you sound and look more confident and believable.

Ask For This

21

Get Discounts Galore

You can wait for something to go on sale and risk not getting the item you want or you can ask for a discount at the time you need the item. Preconceived notions about where and when you can ask for a discount are keeping you from getting a better deal. Not sure what to say? Try these practical suggestions on how to ask for a discount.

Ask for a discount now

Don't wait. By waiting you take a chance the price could go up, the store could run out of your size or the product could disappear from the shelf. What good is a sale when all that's left are size XXL and you wear a medium? Give store personnel a good reason why they should give you a discount on the item you want today. You could be a regular customer or you might have a lingering customer service issue. That good reason is their WIFM for granting your request.

Example

Suppose you've been shopping for a specific item and instead of waiting for it to go on sale you decide to ask for a discount. You have periodically checked to see how long that item has been in the store. Unusual or one-of-a-kind items that don't move aren't making any money for the owner or manager in charge who could use the same space for more profitable merchandise.

First, you ask who has the authority regarding price changes. Tell the manager (or owner) you've had your eye on the item and mention how long it's been gathering dust. Ask if you can take it off her hands at a discounted price and see what happens. Your request could sound like this, "I see you've had this cooler on your shelf for three months and it looks like it's collecting dust up there. It's kind of a funny green, but I've had my eye on it and I'd be willing to take it today if you'd be willing to give me a discount. May I buy it for twenty-five percent off?"

An alternative is to ask for an unspecified discount and listen to the response. The amount could be more than what you anticipated. If you don't think the discount is high enough, you don't have to take it. Your refusal might prompt a better offer. You can also make a counter offer.

The non-fatal flaw

You can ask for a discount on a non-discounted item when you find a flaw in it. A new sweater may have a tear in a seam, something you could fix at home. You take a chance with make-up smears and other stains. They may not wash out. Check for something irregular about the sweater that may have been missed in quality control such as an uneven seam or a missing button. These are bargaining chips you can present to the salesperson or manager. You're willing to pay less for the item; they off-load a piece of damaged or irregular merchandise. This is a win-win and can also apply to floor models, demos and items in crushed packages.

Decide ahead of time what you'd be willing to pay for the damaged or imperfect product and ask what they'll do for you. Ask for discounts on items missing a non-essential or replaceable part. That part costs money should you decide to buy it elsewhere, so you need to take that into account.

Example

"Excuse me, this file cabinet is missing the key to the drawer and it looks like the last one of its kind. It'll cost me money and more of my time to replace the lock or to get a key to fit. What sort of price adjustment can you give me?"

It doesn't matter whether the item is already discounted; you can ask for a greater discount. Don't assume the flaw is the reason why the item was discounted in the first place. It could have gone unnoticed.

Blems

Take advantage of slightly imperfect items by asking for one with a blemish or "blem." Blems can be purely cosmetic, such as an uneven textured surface. A small dent in the back of a dryer that has no impact on its usability could bring a hefty discount and you'd never see the flaw. When you find an appliance that meets your needs, ask the store where they keep their slightly damaged items. They may tuck these away out of sight in a separate warehouse or outlet center where blems or seconds can be purchased. Be absolutely sure there is no change in the warranty or the item's utility.

JoAnn went to a national home remodeling chain store to buy a barbeque grill for her patio. Most of the ones they had were too large. She looked around until she found one the right size. It was the only one available. The grill had a noticeable ding on one side and was already reduced from $200 down to $120. JoAnn pointed out the ding to a salesperson and asked for a further reduction, which was declined. The store delivery charge was $80, more than JoAnn wanted to pay, and because she couldn't handle the grill transport herself she *asked for a reduction in the delivery charge. She was told no adjustments could be made. JoAnn thought the total was too much and was prepared to drop the purchase. At this point, the salesperson agreed to discount the grill an additional $50 and JoAnn agreed to take it.*

At the supermarket

Another way to take advantage of slightly damaged merchandise is at the supermarket. Crunched, but usable boxes are usually on a sale rack in the rear of the store along with discontinued items. That doesn't mean the employees catch everything. Personally, I don't trust dented cans, but there's nothing suspicious about a cereal box with a slice across the top as long as the inner bag is still properly sealed from the factory. Point it out and ask for a discount.

Good things to ask are:

- "Where do you have your discounted items?"
- "Do you discount day-old baked goods and where are they kept?"
- "Do you discount older produce?" – for example, over-ripe bananas that could be used to make banana bread.

Is your market batting zero? Ask if they have a program in place to donate usable items they would otherwise toss. If they're not going to the general public, food banks and homeless shelters gladly accept these items.

Bulk discounts

Bulk purchases at warehouse stores usually provide substantial savings, but what about buying in bulk elsewhere? Remember, you don't need to wait for a sale. Call ahead of time when possible and ask management for a bulk discount based on either the large number of items you plan to buy or a percentage discount based on the total dollar amount. You could ask for your order to be prepared ahead of pick up – a great way to save both time and money.

When you repeatedly purchase an item, ink or toner cartridges for example, ask how you can get discounts over time in a frequent buyer program. You may be able to add up your purchases over the course of a year, as opposed to the smaller sales you're making from time to time, and qualify for a discount.

Membership and store cards

The stores in your area may not be actively advertising all their available promotions. Ask what programs are current. Ask how to enroll and start racking up points toward a future discount. If a store asks for your e-mail or home address for their mailing list, ask if there is a benefit to you by signing up right then. Besides a discount or a coupon toward a future purchase, you might get to take home a freebie you never would have gotten otherwise.

Many department stores offer a discount for signing up for a credit card at the time of purchase. Ask for one if they don't offer. Obviously, the more you buy, the more you save that day. Don't waste your discount on an insignificant amount. Some stores extend the time in which you can make your purchases and still have the discount apply. Ask what the best deal is for you before you sign up.

Remember, your credit report includes your store credit cards and their limits. Too many open cards can lower your credit score. You wouldn't want to pay more in interest on a significant loan because you got some smaller discounts at department stores. Department store credit cards charge interest similar to those of major credit cards. Your discount will quickly vanish with the interest you are paying on these accounts. Keep this in mind when thinking about how much you are saving. Or, ask if the store has a free layaway program and forgo credit altogether.

As part of the greening of corporate America, many stores will give you a discount for providing your own bags, while others charge more for providing you with theirs. Some stores give you an extra discount when the reusable bags have their name on them. Ask your favorite stores about their policies. Ask yourself to remember to keep a few reusable bags in your car.

You may possess a membership or store card that enables you to purchase items at specific stores at a predetermined discount. Forgot to bring in your card? The cashier may be able to key your phone number into the checkout computer to give you the discount. Be sure to update this information when you move. One year I saved enough money buying expensive, higher quality house paint to pay for the difference in the cost of the paint and my yearly roadside service membership that enabled me to get the discount in the first place.

Rebates

A rebate returns money to you. This usually involves filling out a form. Store advertisements play up the extra savings you receive after rebate to entice you to buy, but then don't always have the rebate paperwork handy. Check expiration dates and send in your form before the required post-marked date or your discount will disappear. There's no guarantee your rebate check will arrive in one week or eight. I've heard of cases where rebate checks never arrived when the requirements were supposedly met. Then whom do you ask for your money? Instant in-store rebates are great – no waiting, no fuss, no doubt!

Crazy for Coupons

After their use trailed off during better economic times, coupons are once again hot commodities. Have you used a coupon lately? They arrive in your mailbox, newspaper, magazines, newsletters, cell phone, and on the Internet where you can print them out. They're handed out inside stores, at trade shows and other events. They come stuck to the product where you can peel them off and use them immediately. You and a buddy can trade unused coupons. Ask like-minded friends to join you for coupon swaps.

The big type giveth and the small type taketh away

It can be hard to read the type on a coupon. You may need to ask what it says to be sure you're getting the right item. You might think the coupon is good only for the featured new product, when the coupon states any product by the brand will suffice. A store name may be printed on a manufacturer's coupon, but you should be able to use it at a different store that takes their coupons. Restaurant coupons may only be good during non-peak hours and not valid on holidays or weekends. Some coupons apply to first-time customers. Ask. Oil change coupons may be good for one grade of oil or not apply to all car makes. Your coupon may save you a certain percent not to exceed a specified dollar amount. Or you may have to buy two of the item. The coupon may be good only at select locations. Ask if you're unsure.

Expired or misplaced coupons

Businesses vary in how they treat expired or misplaced coupons.

They aren't obligated to honor an old coupon and you aren't obligated to use their services or buy their product. Don't let a forgotten or expired coupon render you helpless. Ask to have it honored anyway. Sometimes the store will have a flyer with a coupon in it they will let you use to ring up the sale. Specials change. You may qualify for a new offer. Ask what's available and ask for a similar service or product when the one advertised is not right for you. If you want a sold-out item, ask for a rain check so you can buy it at a later date. Also ask about limits to the number of the products you can buy at the special price. There are businesses that will do whatever it takes to make you a customer including honoring their competitor's coupons. Ask whether this is their policy, and if it's not, ask if they'll honor it anyway!

Example

- "Will you accept this expired coupon?"

- "Do you have an extra store coupon I can use for this item?"

- "This coupon is for permanent hair dye only. Will you honor it for the highlighter kit?"

- "Do you honor competitor's coupons? What about this one for a free tool sharpening?"

Other great things to ask:

- "Does your store take all coupons?"

- "Do you ever offer double coupons? Is there a limit?"

- "Am I able to use the store coupon in addition to the manufacturer's coupon?"

- "I don't have a coupon. Will you give me a discount anyway?"

- "Does your store have some kind of a points program where I can earn coupons?"

At my local bowling alley you can get coupons for future games – usually buy one, get one free. They hand them out only after you've finished bowling. You have to ask for them and sometimes that means waiting while they help incoming customers. The attendants who know me are more generous with the number of coupons they hand out than the new employees. On occasion they've been known to honor expired coupons or grab a current one to help me out. Once I ran into the weekend deejay before his show. He asked me an easy trivia question as an excuse to hand me a free game coupon. At the counter I refer to the employees by their first names and ask them how they are. During the holidays, I let them know how their good customer service makes bowling more fun. It pays to know your local businesses and to give back in ways folks appreciate. You give, you get.

Do a coupon search

Don't wait for your favorite product to come out with a coupon. Go to the company's web site and look for their fan club, newsletter or membership sign-up where you will be eligible to receive coupons. You can get coupons for restaurants, products and services not normally found in print. If a sign-up is not available, contact the company by e-mail or phone (look for a toll-free number on the product's container) and tell them you would buy their product or service more often with a coupon. Requests from a few customers are usually all it takes for a company to wake up to this missed sales opportunity. Calling or writing the company with a product review – irrespective of whether you give a complimentary or poor rating – is a good way to get coupons and free samples, especially when you come right out and ask for them.

Marty loves all kinds of berries and buys them from her local markets. On one trip, she bought a large six-dollar container of blueberries labeled with a familiar brand and was disappointed in the mushy quality. They looked good through the sealed plastic clamshell and from past experience knew they could be delicious. The company web site was printed on the label. She wrote a courteous e-mail expressing how her previous delight with their product led her to purchase the large container that proved disappointing. Marty let them know she would buy their berries again and deliberately ended the note with an open query for resolution. In short order she received a nice letter back apologizing for the quality along with ten coupons for sixty-cents each – a total of six dollars savings for all the coupons.

The berry company responded with coupons even though Marty had never seen any before for this brand. She could have suggested a remedy or just sent them the e-mail as a reminder to watch their quality control. By asking them how they would like to resolve her disappointment, she left the door open to possibility. They could have sent a refund check, coupons for berries or another one of their products, sent actual product, sent a claim form asking for her cash register tape, sent a written apology, sent a booklet on how to buy fresh fruit, had someone from customer service call, or some other option. Of course they could have ignored her e-mail and potentially lost a customer. They were smart and didn't let that happen.

Drive Your Best Car Deal

In mid-life, I chose car sales as a career. My family and friends thought I was nuts. Good thing I didn't listen to them because I did very well and had a good time doing it. I sold both domestic and import models and later became a finance manager, settling in at a high-end import dealership.

As I moved up the career ladder, I heard the same expression in various forms over and over – *you don't ask, you don't get!* This applied to the dealership operation and employees as much as to the customer. I used this philosophy in other areas of my life. Friends and family heard me say it and use it. Then they began to say it and use it. I'm working toward a viral success story of global magnitude for *You Don't Ask, You Don't Get,* and I have the car biz to thank.

I've seen a lot on the lot and could write a book on this subject, but that's for another day. *You Don't Ask, You Don't Get* is about asking for what you want, so I'll share with you some of the better car-buying questions.

Interview

The next time you plan on buying a new or used car, begin by interviewing your friends and family. Ask them for recommendations. Ask them everything you want to know about the car and the deal. Keep in mind not everyone wants to discuss finances. Ask:

- "Do you think your salesperson was honest and forthcoming with information?"

- "Do you like the dealership or agency?"
- "Why do you like the brand?"
- "Did you use a buying agent or service and what was the experience like?"
- "What do you like and dislike about driving the car?"

Interview people you don't know. Can you do that? Yes, you can. When hybrids came out, I'd roll down my window and ask someone at a red light how they liked their hybrid and what kind of mileage they were getting. Express interest and the floodgates open. Strangers will tell you all kinds of honest information they won't admit to people they know. Ask them about likes and dislikes. It's amazing what you can learn in one minute of unfiltered conversation while waiting for the red light to change.

Ask yourself before you shop

Your brother may like his mini-van because it's the right car for him and his family. You have to decide what's right for you. Analyze your needs before you shop. Do a lot of research on-line. You'll still have plenty of questions once you get to the agency. Ask yourself:

- Who will be the main driver(s)? What are their needs?
- How much will insurance cost for the few vehicles I'm considering? What lowers the rate?
- What kind of gas mileage and maintenance can I expect? How does that fit into the budget?
- How long will I keep this car?
- WIFM? Practical? Status? Emotional? Is WIFM worth the trade-offs?

- Do I understand the difference between what my current car is worth on the open market and the lower value the dealer will give me?

- How many miles a year have I typically put on a car and how might that change?

- Am I best served by doing a lot of the work myself and buying through an agency's Internet department?

Your salesperson

It's okay when first arriving at a dealership to request a male or female salesperson. When you relate better to a specific gender a sale is more likely to take place, a benefit to the dealership and you. Call ahead with your request and you will avoid a potentially awkward moment in person. Keep your appointment, or call to change or cancel.

Hopefully your salesperson is knowledgeable and friendly. If not, you can ask to work with someone else. Assuming everything is okay, put your mouth into gear and ask away. Then, shift into park, be quiet, and listen to the answers.

- Ask anything you don't understand about the vehicle.

- Ask for a test drive that includes roads and speeds typical for you.

- Ask to see the car in broad daylight or you might end up buying a purplish car you thought looked blue under the low-vapor yellow lot lights. (That guy and his wife were not happy the next day.)

- Ask about the possibility of taking the car for an extended drive or keeping it overnight.

A simple test drive may not be enough. The agency may allow you to sign a borrowed car agreement. For example, a woman came to the dealership concerned about seat support. She explained how a long drive in some cars caused her back trouble. I arranged for her to take the car home. She spent several hours sitting in her driveway reading a novel until she felt sure a long drive wouldn't aggravate her back. She returned the next morning and bought the car. Also, renting a car is an inexpensive way to find a model right for you.

Wheeling and dealing

Agencies with fixed price tags offer vehicles at a slight discount. There is no negotiating. You take it or leave it. Ask around to find one that represents the model you like. Otherwise, be prepared to negotiate. The dealership is not going to wheel and deal unless you start the process.

A friend of mine assumed the salesman was negotiating on her behalf when he went to get numbers from the sales manager. This did not happen because she never asked him to do it! He merely provided a monthly payment based on a suggested down payment. She paid full price for the car. She showed me her paperwork two days after her purchase and wanted to know what I could do about it. Duh! Why didn't she let me know ahead of time she was buying a car? She didn't want to bother me before the purchase. It was incredibly frustrating. I wished she had asked me the week prior.

Financing

Do your homework on-line and at your own financial institution before you go to the car lot. It helps to know ahead of time what financing is available so you can compare. Know the difference between buying and leasing. You don't have to take the dealer's financing, but your bank can't touch 0% or a heavily subsidized rate. You may not be aware of all the particulars the dealership offers. Ask your salesperson, sales manager or finance manager to explain what's available. You should know your credit score before you go, even though the dealership will run your credit too. Ask to see it if questions arise about your accounts. You can get a copy of any contract to read before you sign.

For leasing ask:

- "What's the lease money factor and how does it compute to a comparable interest rate?"

- "What is the residual amount, and which extras can be residualized?"

- "What are the options for yearly mileage and what is the penalty for going over?"

- "Is it an open-ended or close-ended lease?"

- "Is a 39-month lease still less expensive after you add in an extra year's registration renewal?"

- "Does it make sense to sign a pre-paid lease?"

- "Are there minimum or maximum limits on the down payment?"

- "What is expected at lease end regarding the condition of the car?"

- "Can I turn the car in at a different location than where I bought it?"

For retail financing ask:

- "What are the payments for three-, four- or five-year terms?"
- "Are longer terms available?"
- "Is it a simple interest contract?"
- "Have they added in anything other than the price of the car I'm buying?"
- "Is a down payment necessary? And if so, what is the minimum amount needed for my credit score?"

General questions you can ask:

- "Where is the paperwork that spells out other agreements we've made?"
- "Is there a return policy on new or used cars, and if so, how much does it cost and what are the details?"
- "What is the warranty on the used car I am buying, how long is it good for, what does it cover, and who can do the repairs?"
- "When is the registration due on the used car I am buying?"
- "Have I received a copy of every paper I've signed?"
- "What's the highest allowable credit card charge you will accept?"

You may also want to check with your credit card company for their limit as well. You can let them know you are buying a car and ask for a higher limit.

Trade-ins

The dealership is not going to pay anything near retail for the car you've been driving. At best you will get wholesale. Most likely, you will receive one to two thousand dollars less than wholesale on a car you believe is in good condition. Be aware that most folks overrate their car's condition. On a rare occasion, a dealer will give you time to sell your car on your own, and if it doesn't sell within a specified time period you trade-in your old vehicle for an agreed upon price. Otherwise, you will bring in the same amount in cash. Ask about it.

Good trade-in questions to ask:

- "Will you show me a printout of my car's wholesale value including the extras on the car?"

- "Will you be wholesaling my car or selling it on the lot?"

- "How much will the value of my trade-in increase if I have certain things fixed?"

- "Do you offer consignment privileges on your used car lot and what is the premium?"

Aftermarket items

Don't forget to do your homework when it comes to vehicle aftermarket items. Ask if you can get your extras such as window tint, CD changer, or alarm installed before you pick up your car. Ask to read the contracts for extended service, maintenance and/or tire protection package ahead of time. Ask whether these extras can be added into your retail/lease contract.

A family member went car shopping and followed my advice along the way. Near the end of negotiations she called me to ask if I thought the dealership would throw in window tint to close the deal. Up until then she hadn't mentioned window tint and I asked if that was important to her. When she said "No," I questioned the benefit. She wanted something extra

*to feel more strongly she had squeezed everything she could
out of the deal. I told her to forget the tint because it held no
value for her. Her emotional and financial WIFM surpassed
the practical aspects of the deal, which were already in place.*

Service department

Your salesperson may have agreed to give you a loaner car when
you come in for service. Get it in writing. It may be the current policy
of the service department for certain longer services, but policies can
change. If it's not in writing, it isn't happening, not for you and not for
them. Verbal assurances aren't worth the paper they're printed on.

On a slow day you may be able to get a loaner car when you
ordinarily wouldn't get one. Make an appointment and while you're
at it, make your loaner request ahead of time. Ask if their loaner cars
are free. Ask about their shuttle service too.

Your service writer works on commission, just like your salesperson. When he recommends a particular service, ask why. Is it a
recommended item in your owner's manual or the dealership's idea
of good service? Decide who gets the most benefit, you and your car,
or the service writer and dealership.

Other good questions for your service writer include:

- "Can you please install protective coverings before the guy
  (with the greasy hands) gets in and takes my car away?"

- "What brand of parts will be used in the repair and why?"

- "Are they O.E.M. (original equipment manufacture)?"

- "Will you set aside my broken parts for inspection before I
  pick up my car?"

- "How long do you warranty parts and service for each repair item?"

- "Do you wash the car as part of the regular service?"

Ask your service writer about providing fix-up/clean-up/detail services for your older vehicle. They may be able to fix the leather tears on your car seats or smooth out a door ding while your car is receiving other maintenance. Allow extra time for these services.

Auto Body Shop

Much of what you would ask your service writer also applies to auto bodywork. Your insurance company may be footing the bill, however that is no excuse for poor workmanship. My car was damaged in an employee parking lot by a co-worker who paid the bill. The work was done on the premises and I wasn't happy with the orange peel finish. I asked that the job be redone and it was.

After the sale

A good salesperson is there for you after the sale, but that doesn't mean you can ask for the world. He may set your radio stations and add a dozen phone numbers into your hands-free system, but don't expect him to tap in your entire phone book. Your salesperson can handle small requests like missing floor mats or your NAV CD. He may turn you over to another person when departments are separated. This isn't an affront to you; it's the way the agency delegates responsibility. Rather than expect your salesperson to be the only go-to guy, ask him whom you should see for specific matters and get an introduction while you're there.

Finally, after you sign the papers enjoy your vehicle. Don't look back unless you think there's been misrepresentation or fraud.

Private sales

Whether you are the buyer or seller, be proactive and your sale will go more smoothly. In most cases, buyers and sellers want and need the same information. Don't rely on the other party to take care of everything. Ask for the sale to be consummated in a public place like your bank lobby or DMV. Visit your local DMV ahead of time and ask which forms you need to transfer a car and how they should be filled out. Turn in the forms yourself. Call your insurance agency and tell them about the change.

Sellers

Make a copy or log each service you've had done to show a prospective buyer. There are web sites that show a car's history. Many are reliable, but only to a point, because not all maintenance work or accidents are reported. Get one anyway. One of the advantages of seeing the same service department is that you can ask for a printout of all the service you've had done over the years.

Clean up your car inside and out. Sounds logical, yet I've spoken to folks who admitted they got less money because they didn't take the time to wash their car before it was sold. Buyers may assume a dirty car is an indication of how the car has been treated in general.

Decide ahead of time where you'll allow a test drive and by whom. Ask to see a driver's license. Jot down the number and leave it in your home before you head out. You may deny a request for another to drive your car. You can do the driving. Your safety comes first.

Be honest about your car's problems. It is, after all, a used car. You have two choices. Either fix your car first and justify your asking price, or be prepared to let a serious buyer take the car to the mechanic of their choice at their cost. A mechanic will point out major and minor flaws. In this case, be prepared to negotiate downward because the cost of car repairs will be borne by the buyer.

Avoid being a victim of fraud. If you don't get cash, ask that the transfer of the vehicle and the title be held until *final* verification by your bank that funds have been transferred. Electronic funds transfers have been known to show up and later found to be nonexistent. Do not give cash back for supposed over-payment from a check or wire transfer for an amount higher than the agreed upon price. Don't let a stranger pressure you into agreements you don't find comfortable, especially if they offer you more money to do the deal quickly.

Buyers

Before you head out to see a car, find out the current range of values for that particular car's year, mileage and condition. Ask for maintenance records and the car's history. Ask for a test drive. Begin negotiations only on cars in which you have a serious interest. Ask your mechanic ahead of time how much he charges to look over a used car and how available he would be on short notice. Ask to see the title ahead of time to be sure there is no lien holder and that the seller has the same name as listed on the title. Ask to see the lien holder's release. Call the former lien holder if necessary to clear up confusion. Ask to see the seller's identification. Match the title to the car's vehicle identification number (VIN).

No two used cars are exactly alike and neither are the situations that bring together buyers and sellers. As the next story illustrates, a fair agreement is limited only by your imagination and the willingness of another to find middle ground.

Trent planned to move from the suburbs to the country where his sports car would have been impractical. At the same time, Ben was moving back to the city and didn't need his older pickup. Trent asked Ben if he wanted to trade cars. The two decided it would be fun and practical. Ben agreed to pay Trent extra to even out the deal. Three days before the trade, the transmission unexpectedly went out on Trent's car. He had no choice but to fix it. Trent had the utility of the transmission for the life of the car to that point, but he also felt the deal was arranged based on the car being used. Ben would now have the advantage of receiving a brand new transmission, an item of added value. Trent asked Ben to split the repair cost, no small amount, and Ben agreed to pay half. The two made their deal.

Internet sales

Many of the tips mentioned above in private sales also apply to Internet sales. On the Internet you don't always have the advantage of buying local and seeing the seller and his car in person. The car in which you have an interest may be a thousand miles away. You may not know of the seller and have to rely on references. Ask for them and make the calls. Do an Internet search to find independent reviews. Use an independent escrow service if necessary. Ask about trucking and insurance costs, clear title, and anything else pertinent to your purchase. Ask your DMV or government office about potential sales tax advantages for receiving your car in your state.

Get More Out of Retail

There is a huge grey area in the retail trade, one allowing you to ask for all manner of things you never thought possible without coming across as greedy, entitled or uncouth. The only thing holding you back is your imagination. You can ask for anything. The term "retail trade" helps put the focus on the exchange that takes place. You want to be sure you get good value for the money you trade. A retail store can trade goodwill and so can you. Being a customer has value. It's a commodity you can use for trade.

You've been trained

Retail stores set a price and you pay it. You accept this system of doing business without question because you've been trained to do so. To refresh your memory about how to bargain at a retail store, see Chapter 16, *Bargaining and Bartering*.

Establishing a set price serves an important purpose. Each retail establishment should know what kind of markup they need to remain in business and they must price their merchandise accordingly. You can't buy the product or service if the company goes out of business. Low profit margins can mean your favorite product could be discontinued with no notice. Then it's up to you to find it at another store or contact the manufacturer to find remaining outlets. Look for a toll-free number, e-mail or web address on the product to ask how you can purchase remaining stock directly from the manufacturer at a bulk discount. You may have to buy half a dozen, a case, or an entire pallet, but it might be worth it to you. Ask about free shipping, or ask them to use inexpensive ground transportation. Ask for the locations of remaining outlets. You may discover the product is being carried in different stores.

Getting the goods

Most folks know they can negotiate on big-ticket items. The good news is you can pick up this type of merchandise at a great bargain. The bad news is that's because some big box stores have drastically cut back and others have closed their doors. Ask yourself how important it is to be able to go back to the store should you encounter a problem. Will their financial troubles make it impossible to get replacement parts in a few years? Ask now about their plans and listen with both a skeptical and an optimistic ear.

In general, it helps to ask the retailer what their plans are for backing up their merchandise. Don't rely on the salesperson's word alone. Get it in writing, although that won't hold much weight if they close their doors forever. While you're at it, ask them why you should buy from them and not the retailer down the street. You'll be amazed at what you can learn.

Example

- "Am I taking a risk by buying the store brand? Who will provide parts when I need them?"

- "Can you explain to me how you back up your merchandise?"

- "Everyone pretty much has the same things. Can you give me a great reason why I should buy from you today instead of shopping around?"

Ask anywhere, anytime

The truth is you don't have to limit yourself to big-ticket items to ask for a special arrangement. Many folks are under the impression that rules are rules when in reality small, medium, large and mega-store chains are allowed to make price and/or policy adjustments. Before you ask for something special, think about why management would be inclined to grant your request. Here are a few good reasons when making your case.

Example

When you are a regular customer:

> "I already bought three of these sofa pillows from you and I need one more. Do you think you could see your way to giving me this one at half price?"

When you have a large or drawn out purchase:

> "I understand why you can't give me much of a discount with my first widget order because it isn't all that large, but we plan on needing a steady supply of these. By December I hope to order enough so the cumulative amount is equal to 5,000, the amount where we'd ordinarily get a break. What I'm asking is that with each monthly order we get an additional two percent discount and that when we reach 5,000 widgets, you credit my account for the difference. Of course I'll pay for the shipping. Can we do that?"

When you have a special requirement about returns that would prevent you from making your purchase:

> *I needed a new pair of glasses and wanted to save a few dollars by using the optometry department at a warehouse store. They didn't have any eyeglass frames I liked, but would*

provide lenses at a slight premium if I brought in my own frames. I found a frame I liked at a private optometry office, however I was concerned that the depth of the frames would be marginally insufficient for my progressive lenses. The optometric office policy stated no returns on special orders. Previously, I had not been a customer. However, merely by asking politely I was able to purchase the frames with the guarantee that if the warehouse store was not able to properly fill my prescription, I would be able to return the frames. I made sure the woman helping me had the authority to approve my request and I got this promise in writing, a simple statement hand-written on the receipt. I also expressed my gratitude. Everything worked out and I saved several hundred dollars.

Remember, people buy from people they like and salespeople like to help out likeable customers. Think about your WIFM and the WIFM of the person with whom you are trying to strike a deal. Coupons, discounts and rebates are great, but don't stop there. You can get more out of your retail buying experiences. Ask for something new the next time you're in a store and see what happens.

Bargain hunting in a retail store

Tags can go missing and stores don't always have accurate logs. When the piece you want has no tag, figure out ahead of time what a reasonable price would be based on similar items in the store before you ask a salesperson or manager. You may be able to point out a similar piece to establish a price, or you may be able to suggest a price you find satisfactory. I've had grocery checkers ask me to guesstimate an item's value rather than hold up the line. A stock clerk can also check the price, which is better than over estimating.

How you pay for your item might make a difference. Retailers are charged a fee on credit card purchases. It's convenient, but knocks a couple of percentage points off their profit. Otherwise it doesn't matter too much how you pay because they'll get their money shortly. Offering cash is not the incentive some folks think. Retailers with a preference for ready cash flow, ones that hide money under the table, or ones having problems with credit card or check fraud may wish to deal in cash more often. After you've made your best deal, ask if you can get an additional discount for paying cash.

Warranties

You may be content with the asking price or discount on an item, but what about the warranty? Additional warranty add-ons are a big moneymaker for retailers and not just for big-ticket items. Instead of paying full price, you might be able to get a free or discounted warranty thrown in as a way to close the deal. Ask for it in your negotiations. Be sure the warranty holds value for you. By the way, not all retailers charge for warranties; some offer it free with purchase.

A few more extras

Have you ever been attracted to a particular store display and wish you could have it in your home? Did you ever ask how you could get it? You might be able to purchase the display from the store or even take it home free after the display time has expired. Ask management for details. They may be able to refer you to where they bought the item.

It's not unusual for a customer to take a quick look around a store and leave because he doesn't immediately see what he wants. This is frustrating for the customer who ends up wasting time running around and for the salesperson who doesn't have a chance to offer assistance. It takes only a few seconds to tell a salesperson why you came into the store. There is much to see and not everything is on display.

- Ask for what you don't see.
- Ask the store to bring in the item you desire and whether you have an obligation to buy it.
- Ask for a referral only when it is apparent the store you are in cannot provide the item you want.

Retail referrals

Your retail referral is an important source of business, which is why there are businesspeople willing to pay you for your effort. Who are these people and how do you find them? The next time you have a purchase experience worthy of referral, ask your salesperson, agent or contact if they have a referral program in place. You may receive gift cards, cash, movie passes or free services when you send other buyers to the places where you do business anyway. Or you could send folks to businesses you like because you want to help these good folks and keep the businesses you like in business – a fine way to show gratitude.

Getting free and low cost stuff

It's amazing how many free services your average establishment offers. You might get free gift boxes, gift wrap, or free gift tags. Free or low-cost alterations. Free steaming for your new item of clothing. Free hangers. Free shoe inserts or shoehorn. Free make-up or cologne samples. Free chocolate samples, cookies, food or drinks. Customer restrooms, baby changing tables or nursing rooms. Baby-sitting services. Free mouse pad. Toner and ink cartridge recycling. Shredder. Free e-book. Free matting with purchase of picture frame. Free appetizer with purchase of entrée. Free engraving. Free jewelry cleaning. Free newspaper. Free carwash with oil change. Free ringtones to download.

How do you find out? It might be offered. Or you could ask. Remember, freebies aren't really free. The cost is already built into the price of goods. Take what is offered or ask for a like substitution. Don't be greedy by taking freebies for your whole family and network of friends. That raises the price for everyone, including you!

Internet shopping

Not all items are in the store. Your favorite retailer may offer goods and specials available only on their web site including free shipping or reduced shipping costs for ground transportation. Most sites have an FAQ page, Frequently Asked Questions. Visit their FAQ page before contacting the company with your questions. Don't assume gift certificates purchased on-line are good in their retail store. They may only be good for on-line purchases. Click "contact us" and ask customer service ahead of time.

Valuable Information

A high-ticket item could be on your wish list. Why not? Owning a gorgeous piece of jewelry, an antique grandfather clock, or piece of fine art can bring lasting value and enjoyment. The piece you buy today could be tomorrow's treasured heirloom. Here are a few things to consider when it's your turn to get something nice.

WIFM overload

Beautiful jewelry, finely crafted furniture, fancy clothing, fine art, or one-of-a-kind collectible items spark many WIFM motivations all at once: emotional, logical, financial, personal, and more. Who can resist? This is one area of consumer goods where emotional and personal WIFM value can surpass the actual financial value because it isn't about need, it's about desire. Siblings squabble over heirlooms in part for their real value and in part to satisfy their sentimentality.

Consider the total package

Even money-savvy folks can be blinded by their WIFM motivations for wanting to own a valuable item. Protect yourself by asking the right questions before you make your purchase or otherwise attain the desired object. Assuming the purchase price fits your budget, ask:

- "Will the item need to be insured and how much will it cost?"

- "What sort of on-going special care is needed to maintain the value and what are those costs?"

- "Is there an applicable luxury tax, yearly registration, property tax or other fee?"

- "Does it require separate security measures or insurance?"

Consider the source

Do you really think you can buy a $9,000 watch for $600? If it sounds too good to be true, it *is* too good to be true! Fakes are everywhere and unfortunately, disreputable dealers are, too. They thrive because consumers want to think they got a great deal. Do your homework and buy from honest, stable sources. Ask for referrals, check with the Better Business Bureau, Internet referral sites, Chamber of Commerce, anywhere and everywhere.

Norma Sue's engagement ring, which she owned for many years, boasted a one-and-a-quarter carat diamond. She decided to add a ring guard, an extra band that wrapped around her existing ring, and went to a chain jewelry store for the purchase. The store sent her ring and the new ring guard to their jeweler to do a little work. Unbeknownst to Norma Sue, the jewelry store was days away from bankruptcy. The jeweler kept both of her rings as payment for other unpaid debt from the jewelry store. Norma Sue and her husband had no criminal recourse because the situation was considered a civil matter. Both are shattered by the loss of the rings. Now, not only are they asking for their rings back, they're asking for legal advice.

It's possible the salespeople who assisted Norma Sue had no advance notice of the bankruptcy filing. A little investigating ahead of time would have revealed the trail of closed stores that preceded this unhappy event. You can do your homework by finding out how many stores in the chain have shut down or if the company is experiencing legal problems. Remember this story when you are considering an important retail transaction.

All that glitters

I've spent some time behind the jewelry sales counter. Believe me when I tell you, rather than ask or expect a certain discount, it's better to understand the quality of what you are buying. Then you know when price and value match, irrespective of the great discount someone is offering. You can do lots of advance homework on the Internet and also ask these questions in a jewelry store.

- "What are the different qualities of metals?"

- "Are these gemstones real, enhanced, or lab created?"

- "Who does your diamond grading and which diamonds come with certificates?"

- "Can you tell me about the cut, color, clarity, and carat weight of diamonds?"

- "Which gemstones hold up better than others?"

- "What is involved in maintaining the piece as far as ongoing care and cleaning?"

Ask all the questions necessary to make your informed decision, including my favorite, "What haven't I asked that I would want to know?" Whether considering jewelry or another high-ticket item, you may also want to:

- Ask for a private showing for a very expensive item.

- Ask for an escort to your car if you've made a sizeable purchase, or ask the store to call mall security to walk you out.

- Ask for a plain paper bag to disguise your expensive purchase.
- Ask for the item to be sent via insured delivery service.

Maintenance, repair and policies

Jewelry is meant to be worn and thus, sustains wear and tear. Some of you are harder on your belongings than others, whether you realize it or not, and jewelry is not indestructible. Pieces you hardly ever wear that just sit in a drawer do not break by themselves, but they can be fixed. Ask:

- "What is the policy for backing up new merchandise and repair work?"
- "What is the return policy?"
- "Is there free cleaning?"
- "What happens if a stone falls out or a watch crystal breaks?"
- "When will a watch need an overhaul and what does it cost?"
- "Who does the jewelry repair and appraisals, and what are their credentials?"
- "What other services does the store offer and what are the current charges?" (Remember that costs change over time.)

Those of you concerned about diamond switches during jewelry repair are probably watching too much TV. For your peace of mind go to a store you trust and then ask for your larger diamonds to be plotted, that is, for the inclusions to be noted and measurements taken. A microscope, not a loupe, is the best way to see inclusions. Repaired jewelry looks different than when you brought it in because it has been fixed, cleaned and polished. You may not even recognize it, which is why you should take a good look at it *before* you send it off.

Sidney took his older, broken dive watch to a jewelry chain store. It was sent out to a watch repair service for a new dial and the entire exterior received a good polish. Unfortunately, it was polished so well, the black paint on the bezel was removed and Sidney couldn't read the indented numbers. He asked for the bezel to be returned to its original condition. It took a few weeks, but instead of filling in the missing paint, the company gave him a new bezel at no charge. Sidney was delighted at receiving more than he thought possible.

Extras

Admit it, you want to save some money or get something for free. Ask if the store is having any giveaways, senior or military discounts, upcoming in-store events or special promotions. Ask for free jewelry cleaning, jewelry cleaner or buffing cloth, gift wrap, gift tag, presentation box, or gift with purchase.

Jewelry stores saw their bottom lines slashed during the economic downturn and you may now have to pay for services and extras once received for free. Ask your regular jeweler about their policies before expecting something for nothing. Your jeweler's first responsibility is to stay in business.

Heirlooms

Not all jewelry or valuables are purchased. Much of it is passed on through family along with other kinds of finery, some rich in sentimental value. Someone in your family may have an heirloom you've grown to love, or perhaps you have pieces you'd like to pass down. It's not unusual for folks to take advance measures to ensure specific family members get certain pieces of jewelry, silverware, furniture and other items to carry on traditions and memories.

Ask your family to sit down with you to discuss your plans. Ask how your valuables will be used to be sure your wishes will be followed. Items important to you may have no meaning to some heirs and yet be highly significant to others. Make sure your desires are stated in writing by including specific explanations in your will or trust.

How to ask for an heirloom

Is there a family heirloom important to you? Some consider it disrespectful or crude to ask an elder for a treasured item whether its dollar value is large or small. Instead of asking outright, one option would be to tell the current owner how much the piece means to you. You could mention how you imagine the piece would be enjoyed in years to come or ask the elder if she wouldn't mind sharing her thoughts on the subject.

I remember hearing a story of a grandmother who sold her valuables. She made the assumption none of her family members were interested in the items because none had ever expressed an interest in owning them and she figured it would be easier to divide up the money. Her family was shocked when they heard everything had been sold, and with the items gone, there was nothing to be done.

Some families welcome open discussion, including what will happen to the property of a loved one after they have passed on. When an heirloom is important to you, don't leave it to chance. Ask if you might have an opportunity to continue to cherish the item, or at the least, let your feelings be known.

26

Restaurant Revelry

Eating out is fun, convenient, and a great way to enjoy meals without lifting a finger in the kitchen. You know the basics. Now add to your restaurant experience by making atypical requests. Here are a few ideas to elevate your dining experience.

When you get there

You may not wish to be seated by the bathroom doors, kitchen, or near the loud birthday party with the guy making squeaky balloon hats. Ask your hostess to seat you away from these annoyances. Or, ask up front for a particular table. Walking into a crowded restaurant can mean a long wait. Ask about the possibility of getting full menu service at the bar. Regular patrons might like a specific table or waitress. You can call ahead and reserve a table even in a place that doesn't take reservations. Loyalty has its benefits.

Before you order

You may have chosen a particular restaurant because you clipped a coupon. Ask if they'll honor an expired coupon. When they're out of the featured menu item mentioned in the coupon, ask if they'll substitute a like item or give you a rain check for another night at the same discount. Ask about switching the printed offer from a free appetizer to a free desert or drink.

Ask how old you have to be in order to receive a senior discount, or young-at-heart to order off the kid's menu. Ask if they honor discounts connected to your membership in specific organizations or clubs. The restaurant may have their own card good for a free appetizer, drink or dessert. Some have punch cards good for a free-bie after you've eaten a certain number of meals. Most restaurants appreciate seeing your coupon before you order to be sure there are no misunderstandings.

Substitutions

You know it's okay to ask for grilled instead of fried, or for a biscuit instead of toast. For those of you wondering what else is acceptable, read on. The key is to think outside the box and to ask yourself what you really want to eat. Ask if there is a price difference for the alternate selection. When you read "No Substitutions" printed on the bottom of the menu, ask if that statement still applies.

Example

The menu offers a choice, either soup of the day or salad. Ask to substitute a dish you'd rather have: baked potato, side of steamed veggies, coleslaw, glass of tomato juice, other available soup, hash browns, roll, garlic bread, sliced fruit, pasta, cottage cheese or any other ingredient or dish listed elsewhere on the menu that could be served as a side.

Other ways to ask for substitutions include asking for the dish to be prepared in a sauce other than the one described as going with the food, or as a low-salt, low-fat entrée. You may request a special meal ahead of time with ingredients not normally found on the menu. Give the restaurant advance notice to arrange for this. Special diets should not be left to chance.

You can even substitute the whole menu. Ever look at a menu and can't decide? Feeling adventurous? Ask if you can order off the menu or whether the chef will suggest a series of courses. This is especially fun when sharing food in an ethic restaurant. When portions are known to be large enough for two meals, ask if there is a split plate charge.

Bring your own

In some restaurants you can bring in your own menu choices. Fishermen and hunters can call ahead and ask if the restaurant will prepare fish or game brought in from the wild, and if so, what prep charges to expect. Ask what their policies are as far as bringing your own cake, including serving fee. Bringing in your own alcohol may be permitted. Ask about a pouring or corkage fee.

Party time

When it comes to a more enjoyable dining experience, restaurants can accommodate your large party more easily when you plan ahead. Ask whether they have a separate room of the appropriate size. Ask if a gratuity will automatically be added to your bill. I've witnessed folks double tip not realizing it was already included in the total. Ask the manager about bringing in your own decorations, music, dance, pets, clowns or strippers. Better to be met with smiles than to be asked to leave. Ask about special treatment and treats for birthdays, anniversaries, and other occasions. The wait staff can help make your day memorable. Discuss arrangements ahead of time to hide an engagement ring in a dessert, attach it to a mixing straw or fold it into a fortune cookie.

During your meal

Servers should be notified when your meal is not up to your expectations. Explain the problem and ask for whatever you need: extra sauce, a redo, the salad with the dressing on the side, or a different entrée. For a truly awful, inedible meal that makes you loose your appetite, ask for an adjustment on your bill. You cannot do this after you've eaten half of your food.

Servers are human and missteps occur. A food spill in your lap should come with an offer to pay for cleaning. Otherwise, ask to whom you should send the bill. Your clothing may be a washable item you can toss in your regular laundry, but that shouldn't stop you from asking for a free dessert for your trouble.

Finding a foreign object in your food is no small matter. Tell your server immediately. Point out the problem and ask what the restaurant will do for you. Depending on the offense, you may get a replacement meal, or you could suggest a complimentary dessert.

Almost twenty years ago while eating at a pizza restaurant inside a Las Vegas hotel, I crunched down on a piece of glass and chipped a small corner off a back molar. I called over my server, who apologized profusely and whisked away the uneaten portion. He offered to bring me a new one, plus dessert, and canceled the bill. Management wrote up the report and advised me on how to submit my upcoming dental claim. After I returned home, my dentist was able to smooth out the rough area. I submitted my bill along with mileage at fifty cents a mile, an amount not specifically discussed beforehand. Did I mention my dentist's office was over sixty miles away? I had moved to the countryside and was not about to start up with a new dentist. The hotel called and questioned my mileage. Given the circumstances, I told them I thought the hotel was getting off lightly. They agreed and paid my expenses promptly.

End of meal

Special flavors from your favorite restaurant can be enjoyed at home. Ask how much they charge for a pint of your favorite salad dressing or hot wing sauce to go. Most folks aren't shy about asking for a doggie bag even in a fancy restaurant, so don't be shy about asking for a separate container for anything served to you that will be thrown out once you leave. Your server may give you a little container of barbeque sauce to go with the ribs you're taking home. Otherwise, ask for it.

Finance Matters

What's your preference: Get more? Save more? Spend more? Give more? Isn't that one reason why you bought this book? This chapter is full of tips, techniques, questions, examples and real-life stories of asking about financial matters. And believe me, finance matters! You can improve your financial picture now. Read on.

Credit Cards

You've probably received notices about special credit card offers available for a limited time. Why wait for the next offer? Pick up the phone and call your customer service representative. Put the ball in his lap and ask for what you want.

Example

"I want to reduce my interest rate on my current credit card. I know there are better deals out there. While I'd like to keep my credit card balance with your company, I plan to shop around and I will unless you give me a good reason to stay. What can you do to keep my business?"

Get creative. Don't let the credit card company dictate their policy as an absolute. Ask about other money saving programs and what exceptions they'll allow. Ask how you can get double points by making purchases at select retailers and how you can stay on top of current programs. Give them a good reason why they should bend the rules, continue an out-of-date program or otherwise help you out.

Pay your bill late and you will be charged late fees. Some companies charge you a late fee for a second month after your payments become current. Call customer service and ask them to remove that fee. It's easier to accomplish when you are consistently current on your bill and happen to slip up one month. They will say you agreed to the fee by using the card after they sent you a confusing small print brochure detailing their policies. Don't let that stop you. Let them know why your payment was accidentally late and ask them to remove all the finance charges.

Before a planned large purchase, call the phone number on the back of your card to be sure you have enough in your account or to check your predetermined limit. Many folks falsely assume that because they have cash in their account to cover the purchase, the debit card will go through. Ask about raising the limit for a specific purchase. You can make the call on your cell phone minutes before your sale is rung up.

To deter credit card fraud, ask for your card to be run in your presence rather than let an employee walk off with it where it will be out of your sight.

Banking

Many large and small banks have been bought by another entity. The name of your bank may not have changed, but did their programs? Expect changes to dribble out after the acquisition. Ask questions relevant to your use, such as:

- Can you get free checking?
- Checking with interest?
- Benefits for using direct deposit?

152

- Money Market with checking?
- Special CD interest rates with new savings accounts?

Ask to take a moment with a bank representative to discuss how your money can work better for you.

Switching banks can make sense and cents. A new bank may offer services more in line with your needs. In addition to the above bulleted points, ask about receiving a premium for opening a new account. Once upon a time, a toaster was a common giveaway; now it's money. Twenty-five to fifty dollars wouldn't be unusual. Open a new checking account with direct deposit and you may get as much as $100! *You don't ask, you don't get!*

Ask how you can minimize or eliminate other bank charges you've racked up, for example, with your ATM card or electronic transfers. Ask about setting up automatic payment plans for your mortgage, car payment and other regular bills to maximize the length of time your money stays in an interest-bearing account.

Elizabeth's bank collects a fee for incoming wire transfers. As a thirty-year customer of the bank, Elizabeth had enough. Using her longevity as leverage, she asked many times for the bank to waive the fee and most of the time they did. Lately, they started refusing. Expressing anger didn't help. The last time she called, she asked nicely and they waived the fee again. She understands the bank has a right to collect the fee, but she figures there is nothing to lose by asking. What will they do – cancel her account? No, of course not.

Credit unions offer attractive financial programs. In many states, anyone can become a member, or you may find the criteria for joining is non-restrictive. Don't assume you can't qualify because the credit union name says teachers, Marines, etc. Ask how you can join.

Equity lines and loans

Remember when equity lines of credit were all the rage? You can still get them. Ask your bank or credit union about a secured line of credit. Be careful – late payments can lead to the repossession of your secured item: your car, boat, even your home. Those with high credit scores may be able to get an unsecured loan. Ask how much you may borrow on your good name and payment history.

Not all car buyers are happy with the interest rate on their loan. Ask about refinancing from the lender. The dealership seldom carries the paper. An improved credit score with a new history of on-time payments will increase your chances for success at obtaining a secured loan at a lower rate. Rates fluctuate. Those who initially got a good rate may also improve their loan terms.

Mortgages

You can save lots of money by entering into a mortgage with your mouth wide open in the ask position. How long you plan to stay in your home or keep your mortgage will determine if paying points up front with a lower interest rate is better than paying no points and having a higher interest rate. Do research, or ask your loan consultant if he can do sample calculations for you to determine the difference over a stated period of time. In either case, ask the consultant or lender to remove so-called "junk" fees, such as the "origination fee." Ask whether the bank or agency sells their mortgages to another lender.

The bold among you can ask your loan consultant how much of a cut he is getting in terms of points and/or dollars. Your loan consultant is entitled to make a living, but trimming the excess is part of negotiating a good rate. Many people feel embarrassed to ask this question and your loan consultant may balk at your unabashed candor. Your embarrassment might turn to anger if you found out two points were being added to your mortgage rate. That's a hefty commission, one your loan rep would not want to admit. Check an old title report and see what the bank took the last time – it's on there, or ask folks you know well to explain their title report before you see yours.

You will think a forest was sacrificed to create your paperwork.

- Ask anything you don't understand on your preliminary title report.

- Ask your loan representative anything you don't understand on your loan before you sign.

- Ask about missing information, and to see a revised statement after the missing information has been put in.

- Ask if there is a pre-payment penalty, and if so, how it's figured.

- Ask your loan officer to give you enough time during your appointment to explain everything so you don't feel pressured to sign something you either don't understand or seems incorrect.

- Ask about the cost savings between splitting your payment in half and paying twice a month versus paying once a month. You can do this on your own. It isn't necessary to have it stipulated in the mortgage.

- Ask about the interest savings you would receive by paying a little extra principal with your payment, and also how to make a full payment in advance.

- Ask the best way to arrange for your own notary to come in and pay actual costs, i.e., by the signature as opposed to paying more for the convenience of using the notary the title company provides.

The answers to these questions can help save you thousands of dollars!

Creditors

You've made purchases and now you owe more than you can pay off in a month. You may still have time to return unused merchandise for a refund. Call the store and ask about their return policies. Showing up in person with the item in hand is even better. Give them a choice between potential slow-pay or no-pay versus receiving the item back in like-new condition. That's their financial WIFM.

It's not always possible to return something, a trip to the chiropractor for example. Your chiropractor wants to get paid. Before you make your next appointment, explain your circumstances and see if she will accept reimbursement from your insurance company as full payment. Be upfront with accounts receivable as soon as you experience financial difficulty to work out a payment plan. Ask about the possibility of making a minimum payment of twenty dollars a month to ward off late notices. They want your money and will work with you. Make good on your promise. Consider barter.

Customer loyalty counts and after years of patronage you may see a payoff in ways you had not anticipated. You can ask for a complete deferral of payment for a limited time. Most individual creditors would rather have you pay a small amount and eventually pay off your debt than have to turn your account over to collections where they will get cents on the dollar. Temporary financial setbacks can be overcome, and your positive attitude and good-faith effort will help you get what you want.

You can use your goodwill to advantage in other ways. Have you always been current on your store account? Ask for 0% interest on your next credit purchase. They may have an interest-free or reduced interest plan as part of their regular, but less advertised programs for previous customers or those with excellent credit.

Workplace

Hopefully, your employer has a competent human resources/benefits department where you can go with questions. Ask for a time to meet with HR. Write down your questions and be sure to follow up. Companies change insurers and laws change. That means benefits you've come to rely on can change.

Travis had a job with domestic partnership benefits. His partner, Mike, was unemployed and making COBRA insurance payments. Travis's insurance cost more than what Mike was paying so they kept their insurance separate. Later, Travis's employer switched insurance companies. Travis asked what the new premium would be if he added Mike. He was happy to discover that not only had his premium been reduced, but his employer would pay 35% of the premium for an added domestic partner.

It's not unusual for some folks to pay out-of-pocket expenses for job related activities. Ask your HR department how you can get reimbursed. Unreimbursed expenses may be eligible income tax deductions. Keep receipts and accurate mileage records for all expenses.

Make sure your withholding and other deductions meet your wishes. Do not hesitate to ask about changes in deductions relative to your age, or for a change in income or personal property. Ask for a general review to refamiliarize yourself with paperwork you filled out years ago.

Accountants and money managers

Be proactive and ask your accountant what types of expenses can be considered at tax time. Items legitimately claimed cost less by the percentage of tax you pay and could influence your buying decisions throughout the year. Think you can't afford a tax accountant? Interview one and ask about typical savings. The amount you save could cover the bill and more.

Ever been to a financial seminar with a "free" lunch? You think it's about you, but it's more about the seminar holder's WIFM. One question no one ever asks is, "What's your commission if I buy this annuity?" That's not to say an annuity isn't right for you, or life insurance, or a stock pick. My point is the cost of your financial product is not limited to the fund itself, but includes management fees, commissions, and other fees that eat into your potential profit. When your money manager calls and asks you to switch funds or stocks, ask yourself if it is consistent with your overall financial strategy. Your broker may only be concerned with his commission. Ask if you will incur a tax penalty for selling too soon. Likewise, when interviewing a money manager, ask if commissions are taken on every sale. Some are paid only for their time.

On the home front, have you ever had a financial discussion with your partner? You both have to know what to do and what to expect should one of you die or become disabled. Ask "when" not "if" you can sit down and start talking. Some folks find it hard to initiate this request. Read up on the empowerment section of this book, or if numbers truly muddle your brain, ask a trusted third party to assist.

Utilities and other bills

Homeowners know mortgage interest and property taxes are legitimate year-end deductions. It may be possible to add a city bill, e.g., sewer, to your property tax, a move that could save you money. Ask your city if this is permissible and how to do this.

Incomes change. You may qualify for discounted utility programs formerly overlooked because your previous combined household income was too high. Call the customer service number on your gas, electric, phone, water, and sewer bill and ask what programs they have available for limited income residents. Not all agencies ask for proof of income, but expect to sign papers attesting to your low-income status.

Phone companies are always coming up with package deals to get you to switch over. Don't wait for special offers to show up in the mail. Check the Internet, or call and ask how they plan to bend over backward to get you to sign up.

I rarely watch TV and decided to downgrade my cable service from expanded to basic cable. I called customer service and told them what I wanted. They offered me a six-month extension of my expanded cable for half price. I accepted. At the end of the six months, my TV habits had not changed so I called again to downgrade to basic. Not three weeks later, my cable company called and offered me expanded cable, music, and movie channels for six months for a twenty dollar cable box fee and a dollar and half extra a month over the basic rate – a mere pittance. I accepted their offer again. It's amazing what companies will do to keep your business. Sometimes you don't have to ask. They want your business and they come to you.

Career Benefits

What do you want out of your job or career? A good place to start is to ask yourself how happy you are with your current position. Does it provide sufficient WIFM rewards, or would another choice be better?

That was then, this is now

Your career direction after high school or college was based on life desires at that time and may not be current. Ever wonder why corporate big-wigs leave their fancy desk jobs, the ones you'd die for, to join the Peace Corps? Their financial WIFM was probably overtaken by their strong belief system or a change in personal goals. Hours on the job may have become overwhelming, and aggravated stress levels could have reached an untenable peak. Wherever you are on the career ladder, you can make your new career decision based on the strength of your WIFM motivations today and into the foreseeable future.

Happiness on the job isn't always related to income, though granted, that's a valid concern. If you are unhappy for reasons unrelated to your career, a job change puts you into a new environment where you may continue to be unhappy unless you make changes in other areas of your life. A better work environment could also be the pick-me-up you need to keep charging ahead down the road.

Get your foot in the door

Employment seekers are advised to network as much as possible.

Does your network know you are looking for work? Ask yourself which of these is more important: to find a job quietly on your own or to risk potential embarrassment over letting others know you are out of work. Inside information and contacts can make the difference between getting an interview and having your resume added to the pile. Let the human resources manager know you spoke with a certain individual who suggested you apply. This extra connection is like word-of-mouth advertising and acts as an implied recommendation.

Ask for what you want

Before you were hired, you had an opportunity to ask for all manner of perks along with your salary or hourly wage. It's harder, but not impossible, to ask for extra perks after you're hired. Some jobs offer more than others. How many of these did you ask for?

- Perks in lieu of compensation
- Gas allowance, company car, paid tolls, parking fees or reimbursement for public transportation
- Possibility of telecommuting one or more days a week
- Extra vacation days, specific days off or unpaid leave
- Stepped commission based on performance, a base salary, guarantee, bonus or signing bonus
- Stock options, profit sharing, or inclusion in a 401K
- University classes, workshops or other continuing education
- Part-time, overtime, flex-time, comp time or job sharing
- On-site daycare privileges or daycare reimbursement

- On-site gym privileges or gym membership
- Upgraded medical benefits, dental, vision, life insurance, and/ or disability insurance

This is a partial list. When you might receive these is also negotiable. It helps to know what others are asking for and getting.

Bonnie worked in the human resources department at a bio-medical start-up company. The engineers she interviewed typically asked for a signing bonus, and the company hired a handful of male applicants in a short period of time. At one point, a woman engineer was interviewed and asked for the same bonus. Bonnie admits that at first, those in HR were surprised, followed by shock at their own reaction. Why shouldn't a woman ask for a signing bonus, and why shouldn't she get the same treatment? You don't ask, you don't get! If the woman candidate had said nothing, she would not have received a signing bonus.

It could be "more perfect"

Having the perfect job doesn't mean that everyday is a blissful romp through the meadow. Tomorrow, you may want something else – a raise, a new desk, a better view, an extra day off or a promotion with more challenge.

Use the company's WIFM to help you get what you want. Work conditions change and technology leads the way. Asking for a PDA or cell phone with Internet could help you perform better on the job. You might need more memory in your computer to work faster or a laptop to take on the road. Ask your boss if he would like you to be more efficient by supplying the needed item and you will have keyed into important WIFM motivations.

Asking for too many things can make you appear needy or greedy. Be sure that your requests are reasonable. To help you tap into the company's WIFM and get what you want, ask yourself:

- Can what you want save the company money?
- Will it save on man hours or otherwise contribute to efficiency?
- Will it make your boss or the company look good?
- Does it provide goodwill or other intangible benefit?

Time, money, energy and appearances are strong on-the-job motivators for the person granting your request. Show your boss how receiving the object of your desire caters to these motivators and it will greatly increase your chance for success. Your request may be something everyone in your department can use. Your suggestion for the team demonstrates your ability to be a team player as well as being an independent thinker.

Make your work environment work for you

The workplace offers opportunity for growth and change because most workers are held accountable and are given increasing responsibilities the longer they are with the same company. You don't have to be high up on the career ladder to make your voice heard. To improve your work environment, request ongoing education for you and those within your circle. Ask the best way to contribute suggestions for the betterment of your department. Inquire about adding incentives for implementing money-saving ideas.

Kathryn held a position with diverse duties including project management. She coordinated work flow with other departments and was frustrated by her co-workers' last minute requests to fit in extra work on short deadlines.

164

Her company held regular meetings where workers were encouraged to present ideas to enable the company to save money and/or be more efficient.

When it was Kathryn's turn to make a presentation, she discussed how the account executives could better manage their work load time requirements by being proactive with their clients instead of reactive. Assents and promises followed, but as projects came and went with scant improvement, Kathryn came to realize neither the account managers nor their clients could do what she requested because they didn't think like her. They understood the concepts, but were unable to put them into practice. She couldn't change her co-workers or their clients, but her co-workers better appreciated why her job included project management. Kathryn's acceptance of the situation helped her feel valued for her skills and brought down her stress level. She also realized that she had to focus on doing her job without trying to catch the mistakes of others. Her co-workers would have to deal with their own shortcomings.

Listen to WIFM together

There are times when it is appropriate to make personal requests, such as when you'd like an increase in pay, special time off, and when you'd like additional responsibilities. You can give value first by offering to do more around your workplace. Don't wait for a directive. Ask how you can help your boss if you're not sure what to offer. When your salary review comes around, you can point out how you've earned your raise by setting yourself apart from co-workers who merely put in their time and left at the end of the day. You've demonstrated how your WIFM is their WIFM.

It is known that workplace stress is higher when levels of responsibility and authority are out of sync. If necessary, ask your boss for an increase in either responsibility or authority to become more effective on the job, and then feel your stress levels improve. Company downsizing may have put you in a position of feeling overworked. It would be easy to use that as an excuse for not adding to your responsibilities. Ask instead, either yourself or your boss, how you might perform more efficiently to reduce your overall man hours and save the company money in the process.

Good fences and cubicles make good neighbors

Relationships between co-workers can result in disciplinary action when one or the other crosses the line of acceptable behavior. Many HR departments issue booklets to all hires detailing harassment procedures. You do have a choice where you work, though in a down economy your options are reduced. Your other choice is to find a way to get along with a difficult co-worker in a way that allows you to maintain your work effectiveness and your personal integrity.

Not everyone is equally socialized when it comes to boundaries. A well-meaning co-worker may not know where to draw the line when you feel your space has been invaded or the chit-chat has gotten too personal. It seems there is always someone who cracks their gum, talks too loud, or eats your candy. What to do? HR may want you to ask your co-worker to refrain from the unwanted behavior before taking further action. You may already feel uncomfortable and not know what to say, so here are a few tips.

Example

- "Bob, you know I don't share your political views, so could you please not bring me into these types of conversations?"

- "Sarah, I don't need to know what you and your boyfriend do. Just keep that private, okay?"
- "Excuse me Kevin, I'm trying to concentrate. Can you please keep it down?"
- "You're so sweet to be concerned about my health, but my doctor visits are private. You understand, don't you?"
- "My clients like having a piece of candy, too. Tomorrow, will you bring in a bag of the individual chocolates you like so much?"
- "Will you please confine your swearing to your office?"

Strike a match

Business partnerships have been compared with marriages because of the close association between the parties. Ask yourself whether you have a meeting of the minds before entering into a partnership. How closely do your WIFM motivations match those of the person you are about to team with in business? Bringing different strengths to the table works to the advantage of both. Matching a partner who believes in being honest to a fault, with a partner who advocates "screw them before they screw you" is a disaster waiting to happen.

Happy good-byes

Starting a new job may seem an odd time to negotiate what will happen when you leave, yet executives sign work contracts stipulating the terms for that eventuality. Others negotiate a termination package during times of layoffs. You could take the retirement package your company offers, or you could ask for more. The company's financial WIFM may be served by paying you off and removing you from the payroll. Ask for a retirement bonus, extended healthcare benefits and anything else of value you'd like or have heard others get. Why not you?

Over the course of her long career, Francine worked for several large Wall Street firms and managed to survive the axe each time the financial sector took a dive. It was hard for her to decide which valued employee would get a pink slip and who would stay, and she never knew if her name would hit the chopping block.

As she approached sixty, she paid more attention to her own retirement. By the time the last bear market began, the company she worked for had already made drastic cuts in personnel. She quietly inquired within her organization to see if any retirement packages might be in the offing and was told it was a strong possibility. She waited patiently, extending her own retirement plans longer than anticipated until the timing was right. Her company once again actively sought those who would voluntarily resign and she asked to partake in the next rounds. She received a bonus, extended health care and an offer to continue as a part-time consultant to finish an on-going project. Not bad for someone who wanted to retire anyway!

You Can Ask

Moving Beyond Resistance

Do you resist asking for what you want because your own objections hold you back? You can gain an understanding by looking to WIFM. Coming to grips with your core issues is the first step to changing the voice in your head to better reflect the person you want to be. Depending on how strongly you believe your self-talk, you may dismiss or justify the examples below that reveal the reasoning behind some common objections. Then again, others will hit home – hard!

Emotional WIFM

In the category of emotional WIFM, it is self-protective to inhibit requests that push beyond your emotional comfort zone. The most common reason folks don't ask for what they want is fear of rejection. Rejection can be devastating, triggering emotions such as fear of abandonment or loss of acceptance or love. It's easy to understand why you would avoid putting yourself in such a situation. Fear is a powerful motivator. It can be a dynamic force or it can freeze you into inaction. Avoidance, however, comes at a cost, a classic case of nothing ventured, nothing gained.

Example

You: (Silence.) *You don't ask.*

Them: (More silence.) *You don't get.*

For several weeks running, Bryan received a couple of calls a week, wrong numbers from the same woman who was trying to reach her girlfriend who had a similar phone number. The woman apologized each time and after a few such calls became chatty. Bryan liked the woman's friendly voice and chatted back. On a whim, he asked the woman if she'd like to meet for a drink and dancing. The woman agreed. They met at a local club and spent some time getting to know one another. Though they didn't exactly hit it off, Bryan got out of the house for a fun evening of dancing and music. It was a welcome change of scene from his home office where he worked alone. Asking a "wrong number" for a date stretched his comfort zone and he was glad he went.

Similar to fear of rejection is asking a question you believe could make you appear foolish or cause embarrassment. Believe it or not, many people embrace rejection, embarrassment and other potentially negative emotions because it strips away a roadblock on their way to success. If you never take a swing at the ball, you'll never get on base.

Example

- "I hate to admit this, but I cannot make sense of this month's bank statement. Can you help me?"

- "I don't speak French. Can you explain to me what some of these menu items are?"

- "Would you go to my senior prom with me? I don't care about our age difference. I'd love it if you'd be my date."

It's not unusual to hold back from asking because you are concerned about what another might think. This has more to do with your WIFM motivation than the other person. Someone may give you permission to ask and if you still hesitate, a stronger reason keeps you quiet. Hold your tongue and the risk of making a misstep is removed. Your silence protects you and also keeps you from experiencing growth. Next time, stretch yourself by asking for permission. Then, follow through with your request.

Example

"If you don't mind, I have something personal I'd like to ask. I know you said I could come to you, but if it's too personal, just say so. You've been through menopause and I'm in the beginning of it. Did you ever have unpleasant physical symptoms? I ask, because, obviously, I'm having some problems. What did you do that helped?"

You can try to protect yourself by avoiding difficult questions that might lead to uncomfortable emotions. For example, hearing the truth can be as hard to stomach as knowing you are hearing a lie. You won't get the bad news or the good news either. Burying your head in the sand or procrastinating only makes it harder later when it's time to face reality. Find a way to approach these situations before they get worse.

Example

- "Honey, you've been acting strange. You turn away from me and you seem more interested in staying out late with your friends. Is there something you want to say to me?"

- "Tell me, Professor. What do I need to do to bring up my grade in this class?"

- "Honestly, boss, which job skills should I be working on to be considered for a promotion?"

Physical/Energy WIFM

You have a good idea of what your body is capable of doing or enduring, though you can't always know if you're up to a physical task until you give it a try. Common sense tells you extreme challenges are best left for those in top condition. Generally, you're not going to ask for something that could seriously hurt your body or make you physically uncomfortable for an extended length of time. Addiction and abusive, co-dependent behaviors defy this category.

If your current physical condition or energy level isn't where you'd like it to be to get what you want, make a plan to improve it. Time passes anyway. What you do with it is up to you. Don't hold back on a request based on your assumption of another person's physical condition or energy level. Ask and let them tell you.

Example

- "Are you up for a short walk?"

- "Will you do me a favor this week and not bring home any desserts?"

- "Please don't ask me to take a smoking break with you. I've made up my mind. I'm going to quit. My new habit is going to be a fresh air break. Care to join me?"

When your request seems impractical or inconvenient relative to how much time or energy it would take, you logically hold off. Again, recognize that you may not have all the information. Expending energy can increase your energy level. It sounds contrary, yet ask anyone who's been to the gym how they feel after working out. If only we could harness the energy created from jumping to conclusions!

Logical WIFM

There's no point in asking for something when it doesn't make sense. Based on knowledge gained through past experience, logic, reasoning, or scientific fact, you decide the probability of success ahead of time when considering whether or not you'll make a request.

Logic states that repetition of an identical action will yield an identical result. How often is one situation identical to another? Unbeknownst to you, something new could have been added to the mix. Keep the door open to new possibilities. You can't know everything. Pretending you do will not help you get what you want.

Those stuck in logic tend to be rigid thinkers. Creativity and an open mind are the antidotes. There are options beyond the ones in your head. It's okay to ask to get the answers you need. Left brain types can try asking right brainers for input and vice versa.

Example

- "I'd like to match up our web developer with someone in the client's Internet department so these two can communicate about what needs to be done. How can we make that happen?"

- "I know you can change a battery in a watch, but can you fix this antique clock?"

Fairness WIFM

When fairness issues hold you at bay, you are unprepared to be equally bound or obliged to another. You may already feel obligated and don't wish to add to the load, or perhaps you sense the other person is already overburdened. You may believe the other person is unqualified to respond sufficiently to your specific request and it would be unfair to ask the impossible. However the situation would play out, the scales are tipped against one of you and asking for something would push things further out of balance.

Fairness and logic cross paths. Do not assume what constitutes balance to you is shared by another. What is fair may not be what is equal. Consider your options without a judgment call. Remove assumptions by asking.

Example

- "You've done so much for me already. Would it be an imposition to ask for one more thing?"

- "Instead of getting a new bike like your sister's, I'm wondering, would you rather have guitar lessons?"

Spiritual/Beliefs WIFM

The depth to which you are attached to your belief system is a good indicator of how your requests will conform to and confirm those beliefs. Deep-rooted belief systems may keep you in check and inhibit you from asking something that will pull you beyond accepted boundaries. Folks with strong beliefs may find they quietly question certain aspects or even the larger premise of their belief system. To reinforce your current belief system, direct your questions to those who believe likewise.

Example

- "Rabbi, can you tell me the basis for this ritual?"

- "Father, I'm confused. Why is it we talk about peace on earth and yet there is so much violence in these passages?"

- "Your meditations bring you a steady calm I can't seem to feel. Am I missing something?"

Spirituality may seem as solid as the earth beneath your feet or it could be as ephemeral as trying to grab a fistful of air. Your relationship with a spirit or higher power is personal, yet guilt is a pervasive inhibitor that may stop you from asking for what you need. It takes persistence and determination to override the internalized voice of a teacher, parent or religious leader. You can turn up your inner voice to reflect new beliefs. When your beliefs create angst and you want to change, practice what you believe and not what others tell you. Take leave from your former spiritual advisor if you think a better answer lies elsewhere.

Example

- "I've heard your church leans more toward my way of thinking. Would it be all right if I joined you next Sunday?"

- "As I've gotten older, I find I'm more spiritual than religious. I'd like to talk to others who feel the same. Do you know of a group, or someone I could contact?"

- "I need a break from the congregation while I figure out what I really believe. Can you honor that and give me some space?"

Personal WIFM

You wouldn't knowingly ask for something that was contrary to your personal goal unless you harbor a secret desire for self-sabotage. Some folks do set themselves up for failure. It's possible an underlying fear of success or failure, or a poor self image could be the reason for your silence. Those with preconceived, rigid notions of how to reach their goal cut off avenues of possibility and reinforce narrow-mindedness by censoring their output.

Wayne had a good job as a scientist. He was handsome, and had fun on a date, but he couldn't sustain a permanent relationship. At his job he had done everything necessary to earn a raise except turn in some paperwork. The deadline passed and he received nothing. He knew of other examples of self-sabotage and he found his behavior puzzling.

In therapy, Wayne learned he suffered from feelings of worthlessness and his WIFM supported his view. He didn't

177

complete his paperwork to get his raise because it confirmed the feelings he had about himself – he wasn't worth it. Likewise, he sabotaged the love he let into his life. It was self-fulfilling behavior. With his therapist's help and medication, Wayne was able to battle his underlying depression as well as his destructive behavior. When his yearly job review came around again he completed the paperwork and got his raise. He felt he earned it and celebrated his achievement.

Part of the personal WIFM experience is your level of satisfaction regarding how well you choose to do a job. On one end of the scale is the person who puts in lackluster effort with an "I don't really care" attitude. Ask yourself what it would mean if you put in more effort. On the other end of the scale is the person endlessly struggling to be perfect. Ask yourself what it would mean if your output was less than one hundred percent perfect. You may know from personal experience that either of these mindsets can cause needless suffering. These attitudes are potential roadblocks to getting where you want to go.

Good questions to ask are:

- "What are my personal objections to asking and what purpose do they serve?"

- "What steps do I need to take to remove the objections I've put in place?"

- "Am I willing to move past the notion that pushing my boundaries is too risky?"

- "How would my life change by taking greater control of my actions?"

Financial WIFM

Are financial considerations your bugaboo? You may believe or were taught that financial discussions are forbidden or inappropriate. Fear of appearing ignorant or foolish would compound if someone took advantage of you. You could go to great lengths to protect your inner psyche when the secondary gain of not appearing foolish is stronger than the primary gain of wanting financial knowledge. You may want proof of value before charging ahead. You're not going to ask for something if you know or believe the financial aspects would be out of line with your budget – assuming you have a budget.

This motivation is not just about dollars and cents. It's about emotions, safety, security, enjoying life, or going on a spree. There are many financial styles, not just savers and spenders. Your style fits your WIFM. Be sure it also makes good monetary sense.

Why not enlist the help of a knowledgeable person, a mentor, coach, or a trusted money manager to guide you along? Admit you cannot know everything. As you read in the previous story, personal problems can also lead to not asking for financial well-being. Give yourself permission to seek help from the right professional.

Practice

When you understand your finances and know your limits, try acting as if you have a little bit more – or less – money than you actually have, to either loosen – or tighten – your purse strings. Note how you feel when both giving and receiving money under these guidelines. It's not just the money. How ready are you to give and receive?

Retrain Your Brain

Not asking for what you want can be habit forming. Habits are produced through repetitive thought and action, or in this case, inaction. You created the habit and you can change it. Some habits fall away without much fanfare. The ones in which you have a large WIFM investment stick around like gum on your shoe. What to do? Retrain your brain.

Here are a few tried and true ways you can work on self-talk plus action to change your habituated thinking. You can make your new self-talk the one you want to hear. This is especially important when you are asking things of yourself or need help in being assertive. When you ask something of yourself, you are responsible for finding the answer. The following techniques should help you with that search.

Affirmations

Affirmations are positive statements that help retrain your brain. Many people like and use them because affirmations work. They are a way for you to speak your new truth. Choose the area you want to work on and write down a positive "I" statement or desired outcome. Post affirmations to yourself in places where you can read them, aloud when possible.

Example

Here are some affirmations for those who struggle with not asking.

- "I can ask for what I want."

- "I communicate my requests effectively."
- "Asking for what I want is consistent with my personal integrity."

You could write your affirmations on sticky notes and place them in your car, on your bathroom mirror, on the refrigerator, and so on. Repeat your affirmations during meditation, when you wake in the morning, before you go to sleep or any time you need a mental break.

If you start to argue with yourself, remember you are worthy of both giving and receiving. It might help to think of a time when you did something for another with no thought of receiving or when someone did something for you with no expectation for the favor to be returned. There are many examples in your life from which to choose: helping a sibling with homework, picking up the family pet from the vet, or letting a friend cry on your shoulder. It doesn't have to be a major event. Many small actions can add up to big feelings, especially when insecurity is at the root of not asking.

Both fairness and personal WIFM motivations are subjective. This means you decide what's fair and what's right for you personally. Exercising value judgments or limitations also come from you and is the likely source of why you prevent yourself from asking. The next time fairness or personal WIFM issues pop up and you hear yourself arguing about why you shouldn't ask, write and then say these affirmations:

- "I deserve to give and receive."
- "I have much to give another."
- "I receive freely."

Do you have a preferred method of practicing affirmations? Great! The point is not so much how you do them, just do them. Try this affirmation: *"You don't ask, you don't get!"*

Say "No!" to Negativity

Unfortunately, there's plenty of negativity out there – in the media, your family, friends, co-workers. It's hard to limit your exposure or to stand up against it when you are constantly asked, either literally or figuratively, to commiserate or add support by joining in the chorus. When you do, you reinforce it. It's a tough habit to break. Others have done it and you can too.

Perpetuating negativity is the opposite of practicing affirmations. Overwhelm negativity with positive thoughts. When you identify negativity in what other's say, resist the temptation to join in. Find something positive to say. Think of this as a new decision. Find a way to acknowledge the feelings of others without putting them down.

Example

To reinforce negativity:

You hear: "Everybody is so rude these days. Why do I even bother?"

You think: *You got that right!*

You say: "No kidding. Everywhere you go, rudeness rules."

To reinforce positivity:

You hear: "Everybody is so rude these days. Why do I even bother?"

You think: *That's a generalization. There are many kind people in the world today.*

You say: "I understand how you feel. Some people are rude. Most of the people I know would go out of their way to help another person."

Remind yourself of this exercise every time negativity creeps in, whether they're in your personal thoughts or spoken in conversation. Reinforce your positive thoughts and they will become more natural as you keep doing it. This can be a silent exercise. When you verbalize, prepare to encounter resistance from those who find it easier to say something negative than to do or feel something positive. They may even say negative things about your new positive attitude! Remember, their comments are a reflection of *them*, not you.

Hold your ground and do what's right for you. There could be times when the prevailing winds blow you backward. Find sanity in the company of like-minded people who have positive attitudes and want to support you. One way to find them is to say something positive and listen to the response. Keep your ears open for people with something positive to say. Spend time with them and whenever possible, separate yourself from naysayers.

It's easier to ask yourself for what you want when others in your circle are supportive. A safe environment will further your goals more quickly than one in which you feel a need to defend yourself. New ideas can be scary. For inspiration, find others who have overcome similar situations. This is why support groups exist.

Good things to ask yourself are:
- "Which areas of my life can use the most work when it comes to removing negativity?"
- "What positive things do I wish to bring into my life?"
- "What positive thought or action can I do today to help make this happen?"

Negativity inspires negativity. It can become so ingrained, you are not aware of how you're thinking, and thus, the way you ask conveys

184

a negative message. A positive outlook inspires others to be positive. Express your ideas in a positive way to positive thinkers and your requests have a better chance at success. Which of the two openings in the following example do you think is more persuasive?

Example

- "I don't know why I'm even asking you about this new idea because it probably won't work."

- "I'm excited about this new idea and I want to ask for your feedback."

If only

In your self-talk, you may play the "if only" record in your head. "If only I had a better job, a steady boyfriend, more money, this, that, or the other thing." Whatever it is, you don't have it. The rest of the sentence goes something like this, "…I'd enjoy getting up and going to work, I'd be happy, I'd start investing." You might be happier if you had more money – or not. This is a vague request. Asking for five thousand dollars is more specific, but the underlying desire could be freedom from financial worry, which might come about through money, education, budgeting, a life-style change or acceptance of your current existence. As long as you decide to play "if only," the longer you can delay having to do anything about your lament.

The "if only" record is a form of self-talk rationalization. It's a way of not having to be responsible for who you are and how your life looks. This type of self-talk reinforces denial and inaction because the blame is placed outside yourself as if it were out of your control.

Playing "if only" is an attempt to shift responsibility – except it doesn't. Saying "if only" is a ploy to get others to sympathize and join your pity party, which may support a WIFM motivation. Believing "if only" takes away your power and places it on something outside yourself. Imagine how your life might change *if only* you took more responsibility for yourself.

To break the "if only" cycle, you can:
- Fight negativity with positivity.

- Use affirmations to help you focus on your desires.

- Act "as if" you have what you want.

- Better define your desires into specific requests.

- Empower yourself by taking control of your life.

- Identify and accept what is truly beyond your control.

Rather than complain about how their lives aren't fulfilled because of some missing ingredient, some people find it helpful to count their blessings. Acknowledging gratitude for what you have is a gift you can give yourself.

Practice

Think of a recent example when you said "If only..." and play out a scenario using "What if... and then..." explained in the next chapter."

Putting the Decision to Ask into Action

Much like the previous chapter, *Retrain Your Brain*, this chapter gives you tools to change habits influencing action. The premise is the same. Identify your old habit and retrain your brain to form a new way of thinking and behaving.

You may know what you are asking of yourself, but not know how to get there. Or, you may have both feet firmly planted in inaction. Ask yourself what keeps you stuck and you will uncover the drive behind your WIFM motivation. Remember, to do nothing about your situation *is a decision*. You can also decide to do something.

This first process can help you sort out your feelings and help you determine your WIFM motivations for continuing on or making a change. It's a pros and cons exercise with a twist.

Pros and cons

Writing out the pros and cons of a situation is a helpful way to sort out your feelings and make a decision. Think of something in your life you consider a challenge or would like to change. It could be to change careers, quit drinking, whether to improve your current relationship, or just about anything else. Write down the habits, actions and/or emotions connected to your current behavior and match them to the WIFM motivational categories that support your thinking. Ask yourself how much weight these points carry. Imagine how you would like to be different, or what you would like to have different, and then write a second list of pros and cons you think would occur should you enact the new behavior.

This self-analysis is only helpful when you are honest with yourself. Those of you in denial will find it harder to fully grasp your true intent. In any case, you can give it a try. You may discover a hidden truth along the way.

Example

Say you've been in a love relationship and marriage is important to you. However, your significant other is in no hurry. Before you bring up the subject to your partner again, you ask yourself if it's a good idea to continue with the relationship, that is, does it meet your personal goals. First, write out the pros and cons of the current situation and the WIFM category, like this:

Pros:

- Partner helps with bills: financial WIFM.

- We love each other: emotional WIFM.

- Partner picks up the kids after school: physical/energy WIFM.

- Partner is good in bed: physical/energy WIFM.

Cons:

- Partner is not the same religion: spiritual/beliefs WIFM

- Partner doesn't always do household chores: physical/energy WIFM

- Partner will not commit: emotional and personal WIFM

- Partner stays out late with friends: emotional WIFM

Four pro points and four con points don't necessarily balance out. Weigh each point separately based on importance. To tip the scales more in favor of the relationship, you can try changing a con point into a pro point by changing your attitude or getting outside help to fill in a problem area over which you have control. You do not have control of your partner, only yourself. You may decide "partner will not commit" counts the most or ultimately is a deal breaker. This point is something over which you do not have control, but this doesn't make you powerless. You may decide to ask yourself: Can you stay in the relationship with no set commitment date, and if so, for how long? Can you accept the truthful answer?

Now pretend you are thinking about breaking off the relationship. Let's assume thus far you have done nothing because you don't want to lose what you have. Have you given thought to what you might gain? Make a second list derived from your pros and write how you might overcome the loss of pro points with positive counterweights:

Pros:
- Help with bills: could get roommate or cut back on extras
- Shared love: could still be friends or keep the relationship at arm's length, opportunity to meet someone else who is emotionally available to commit
- Picks up kids: could carpool with neighbor or have grandparent help out
- Good in bed: you answer this one!

It would be natural to think you wouldn't miss any of the cons. Think again.

Cons:

- Not same religion: used partner as an excuse not to go to church

- Household chores: can do chores the way you like them done

- Can't commit: would miss the time invested in the relationship

- Stays out late with friends: won't hear funny stories from the night out

This exercise helps you grasp the reality that there are pros and cons to everything. Even things you might think of as negatives can have a positive side. It may be a small part of the whole, but it's important to acknowledge it's also a small part of your WIFM. You are benefitting from secondary gains. This explains why you stay in a situation when on the surface it would seem better to do something different.

Working through pros and cons helps you identify your options. Knowing your options helps you act in your best interest. When your self-talk says, "I can't," you may not be seeing all your options. Options are freeing. Options give hope. Options are opportunities. It's up to you to reveal them and choose which ones you want. After you've come up with all your options, give yourself a break. Come back later and think of a few more. If all you see are options you don't like, imagine how you will work through them, or get advice from a trusted source. A few sessions with a therapist, financial planner, coach, or career consultant could help turn you around.

Small steps

Any task, whether large, medium or small, might seem overwhelming with the end result far away and unattainable. Your self-talk says you can't do it. Break down your project or desire into smaller pieces with easier to reach goals along the way. You will create something more manageable and doable.

Example

Suppose you have a home office piled with papers and you've mislaid a check. You ask yourself, "How do I clean up this mess and get some kind of system going so I don't end up with the same disaster three months from now?" This is a big question with several parts. You can find reading materials on organizing, ask a friend how she does it, hire a professional organizer or figure it out yourself. You can mentally pick one of these options, but none of them replaces action.

Keep sight of your primary goal of finding the missing check. It's lost in a pile. You have no idea where to begin. Your WIFM says it's easier to add to the pile than do something about it, making this a WIFM physical/energy issue. Forget the color-coded file folders and the cross-referenced Rolodex. Your first small step is to set aside a *small* amount of time to look for the check, perhaps ten minutes before you start dinner and another ten after the dishes are washed.

Make that ten minutes a priority or you will be stuck in your old WIFM. You may be tempted to sort papers and read old letters. Don't get sidetracked. Stick to your specific task. You may allow yourself to set aside potentially important papers in one pile and old magazines in another, but do not complicate the first task by over-sorting. Focus, keep it simple and keep the step small. Set a timer if you think it will help. Do this again the next day or until you find your check.

Once your first task is completed you can make a decision about the next small step. You could make a priority list, clear out one drawer, gather business cards strewn across your desk into a rubber band, go after the first inch of papers on top of your filing cabinet, or call an organizing consultant. Any small specific task will do. You may decide to take the ten minutes before and after dinner to keep sorting. Though it may be three weeks before you finish, you will finish.

You set a goal and were successful. You found your check. Each ten minutes you take toward your task is a measurable degree of success toward cleaning your office, and also toward developing a new habit. You asked yourself, you got.

What if...and then...

Fear of the unknown can make inaction seem like the lesser of two evils. But is it? Send yourself on a mission and find out. A good way to move beyond your old self-protective mental habits is to explore possibilities in the privacy of your own mind. First, ask yourself a "What if…" question. Answer the question and then follow it with a series of "and then…" phrases. A sample dialogue is shown below.

Example

What if: *I asked my husband if I could bring home a dog?*

Answer: *He'd probably say to forget it.*

And then: *I'd be disappointed.*

(Many folks stop after hearing the first "No." Start a new habit and keep going.)

And then: *I'd ask him why not?*

And then: *He'd say because the house is already crowded.*

And then: *I'd say it could be a small dog.*

192

And then: He'd say it's still too much trouble.

And then: I'd say it would be my dog and I would take care of it.

And then: He might say okay and I'd be happy, or he might tell me to quit bugging him.

And then: I'd feel hurt because sometimes it seems like we have different ideas about how to enjoy life.

And then: I'd be sad for a while.

And then: I guess I'd get over it because I love my husband even though I know he's not a "dog person."

When you've reached the end, ask yourself, "What's the worst thing that could happen?" At this point, any number of thoughts might come into your head related to the different ideas you and your husband have about living life, anything from the loss of love you would give to your imagined pet, the unconditional love it may give you, or that the dog could be a distraction to keep you from focusing on parts of your relationship that need attention. As you can see, this exercise can help you get to the root of the WIFM of your requests. No matter what you discover, if you can live with the final answer, you can ask the question.

While this is a great exercise to try alone, you might choose to practice your question with a friend. As you go along, you will uncover objections. Take the opportunity to decide how you could be proactive or to practice your response should these objections arise when you have the real conversation. This practice session may prompt you to rephrase your original question before you proceed.

No matter the situation, if you can live with the answer, go ahead and ask!

Ask for support

Everyone needs support from time to time. A support group could help you break away the bonds that keep you from asking for what you want. Support groups, whether structured or loose-knit, exist for just about every cause imaginable. Many are free or low cost. Network. Check the Internet or newspaper for meet-ups in your area.

Is there a family member or someone in your circle of friends whose confidence you admire? Ask whether you can buddy up with him or her for an afternoon. Watch and listen when you are together. Ask him or her to teach you how to develop those admirable habits.

Perhaps you know someone with the same goal as you. Ask that person if they'll be your goal buddy. Just like workout buddies at the gym, you can experience progress together and support one another over bumps in the road. Give yourself rewards along the way separate from your ultimate goal.

A mentor or coach is also like a workout buddy who helps you be your best. Retiree groups offer mentoring services, career and business support. Ask your librarian or local Chamber of Commerce for resources. If reaching out for support seems overwhelming, try taking a small step by contacting one person or group and make one appointment. Go to it. Then take your next small step.

Networking groups offer a variety of services and support, e.g., Toastmasters can help you find your voice. If you are hesitant to join right away, ask about the possibility of sitting in on a few meetings without obligation. Many people in these groups remember what it was like to feel silenced and would be happy to lend support as a way of payback to those who helped them. They want to help. Let them. It's part of their WIFM.

Therapy and medical care

If depression or serious mental issues keep you from acting in your best interest, or if what you ask is harmful to yourself or others, please seek the help of a professional. Feeling good physically has a strong impact on how you feel mentally and vice versa. Take care of your health. This book is not meant to be a substitute for proper medical care.

Practice

Think of a personal goal you have put off. Write out the steps to your goal and break each part up into small, doable tasks. Go ahead – take the first step! If you need encouragement, ask for help.

Asking for Too Much or Not Enough

Frequency refers to how often you ask for things. Portion refers to the size of things in your requests. Extremes on either end of frequency or portion are counter-productive to getting what you want. How would you categorize your level of asking in relation to frequency and portion, and what is your WIFM rationale?

Entitlement

When your self-talk filter is on pause and your request meter is on fast-forward, others may conclude you possess an overblown sense of entitlement. Continually asking for all manner of things and favors gives others the impression you are needy, greedy, demanding, lacking in self-control or simply obnoxious. Most everyone knows a "high maintenance" individual, someone who requests one thing after another for their continual comfort. Is this person you?

After weeks, months, and years of piling on requests, you will find it increasingly difficult and eventually impossible to get what you want unless you are dealing with a total pushover. You have a better chance of getting what you want before others feel overloaded by constant requests. If you are not happy with your behavior it's time to hit the mute button on your mouth while you discover more appropriate ways to communicate.

You could tell yourself you don't care what other people think, or find justifications for the number or size of requests you make. Like it or not, those other people are the ones deciding whether to grant your request. When their WIFM feels put out, their output to you will decline or disappear.

When the words *should*, *ought*, *deserve*, and *owe* enter your mind or spill from your lips with regularity, give your entitlement mindset a reality check. Asking your friends or family what they think may provide some objectivity, however it's not unusual to surround yourself with people who either support your views or helped inculcate them in the first place. Consider how you justify your thoughts when you say, "You owe me" or "I'm entitled."

Granted, entitlement implies judgment. What constitutes too much is a personal decision. I don't decide for you and you don't decide for me. Everyone has a different meter on when enough is enough. You also decide the level of comfort you feel relative to how much you ask and whether you want to ramp up or down. Some folks ask for a lot, but also give back heartily.

A sense of entitlement may be a mask that hides your true needs and desires. When you ask for many things, receive them, and still feel unfulfilled, you are asking for the wrong things.

Impulse control

Combine a strong WIFM motivation with poor self-control and you'll impulsively blurt out your wants without thinking first. You may get what you want or your uncensored request may lead to problems. Open mouth. Insert foot.

The advantage of being impetuous is the possibility for instant gratification. Your desire to act spontaneously takes precedence over other factors. You're willing to confront, protest or accept a turndown on the prospect that you might receive a quick reward. Asking in this manner can work for you. It can also make you appear childish.

Long ago, I was introduced to a college student new to my neighborhood. He was heir to a wealthy family and was considered a good catch. He seemed fun and took a liking to both me and my housemate. To help him make friends, we invited him to a party. While there, a woman received a gift of Swiss chocolates from a family member who brought them back from Europe. She offered each of us a chocolate and we all took one. They were delicious, and the young man asked for another. She acquiesced and offered a second round, which the rest of us declined. As we continued to chat, the young man asked for a third, a fourth and finally a fifth piece of chocolate. Her box of chocolates was half empty before the family member suggested she put them away to enjoy at a later date. That young man got the chocolates, but he didn't get another invitation to see us again.

Scarcity

Significant portions of this book are aimed at those who ask for too little. Timid, shy, or quiet folks may miss opportunities by not asking often enough. Are you this person? At some point in time, you made a decision about what you could and couldn't ask for and why. Your beliefs and/or personality keep you and your requests contained. Not asking supports and reinforces your current WIFM.

It's not easy to jump into a fast-paced conversation to ask for something. You might be politely waiting for a natural break in the flow and the next thing you know, everyone else is talking about a different subject, and you and your request got left behind.

You want a good life for yourself. Though you have gotten some of what you want, too often you feel deprived. Much of what we have in life is not given to us. You have to ask for what you want or be prepared to accept less.

Scarcity is a mindset that can linger beyond the point where you have let more into your life. My parents were children during the Great Depression when a lack of resources extended across the nation. Though my father worked into middle-class status, he never lost that sense of scarcity. He hoarded items easily attained or replaced. The items themselves held little value. Nevertheless, beneath the surface the emotions of scarcity ran deep.

Asking can be scary

Are you one to delay your request or never ask at all? Asking can feel scary. Answers are unpredictable and you are reluctant to find out how your request will be handled. It may require demands you would rather not encounter. You temporarily protect yourself by not asking until the deadline is pushed to the edge. Perhaps you tell yourself you had good reason, for example, you got busy with an important project that got pushed forward. If you procrastinate or "forget" to ask until it's too late, you also satisfy your personal interests.

> *Lyndon is a big guy with a shock of white hair and a moustache to match. He looks gruff and keeps his mouth shut. You might think a guy like this throws his weight around to get what he wants, but you'd be mistaken. When he does speak, you quickly discover he's a softhearted teddy bear. For most of his life, Lyndon kept quiet because he felt he didn't deserve much. He is working on self-love to change this notion and has found people who love and accept him as he is now. This helps him strengthen his self-worth from within. Good things and good people have come into his life in the last two years because he has let them in.*

In essence, Lyndon made a new choice. His first step was to acknowledge and take responsibility for his old belief system. Keeping things out reinforced his old WIFM motivations. He is actively changing his belief system by replacing his old self-talk with new loving thoughts that better serve who he wants to be. When he doesn't trust himself, he holds back. It's a slow process, but the results are transforming his life for the better.

Asking for something is a form of reaching out. Don't lose out; stretch your comfort zone. Lyndon did and you can too. You'll be able to use the suggestions in this book to help you prepare and practice.

An attitude of gratitude

Whether you ask for a lot or a little, part of getting what you want includes holding up your end of the deal. It may include money, returning a favor, sharing kitchen duty, or most importantly, giving your gratitude and thanks. Extending these niceties goes beyond good manners. It reinforces your connection with the one that helped you and paves the way for continued positive communication. It gives others a good feeling, an important part of their WIFM. Hopefully, it does the same for you.

Practice

Whether you exercise impetuous self-gratification or self-protection through procrastination, you are tuned in to WIFM. Both of these examples are learned habits. Habits learned can be unlearned. Choose from the techniques mentioned in the last two chapters to help form a new you that better matches who you want to be.

Overcoming Fear

Fear is everywhere. Why? Because fear motivates. This emotion is used in every segment of our society. Parents, teachers, religious leaders, politicians and others in a position of influence or power manipulate it to their advantage. Newspapers, TV, radio, and the Internet employ fear to capture your attention, play on your emotions, and influence your belief systems. Fears move you to action and fears hold you back. Is fear preventing you from asking for what you want and depriving you of living a full, rich life?

Slowing down a reactive response

You may not have the luxury of time when confronted with a fearful situation. However, recognizing fear-based language from others can help you take a step back and not be unduly influenced. Fear-based language triggers emotions and WIFM motivations. In sales situations, you've probably heard expressions meant to play on your emotions to get you to act quickly, like: "You must act now or you'll miss out!" or "Don't put your family in danger a moment longer. Buy this alarm system today!" The hope is that you will respond reactively.

The threat of loss of property, safety, finances, love, and so on, are common triggers meant to get a rise out of you. It's easy to get caught up in emotion. Before you react, give yourself a reality check. Imminent danger is one category in which you must respond immediately. Your boss might also give you a good reason to get moving. Otherwise, don't let someone else push you into hasty action. Practice taking a step back to give yourself the time you need before making your decision. Just because someone puts on the pressure, doesn't mean you have to jump to their tune. You have control over your behavior and your response. Here's how to turn the situation around to your favor.

Example

You: "I like this computer, but it's more than I'm prepared to pay. Is there a way to save on the purchase?"

Clerk: "This is the hottest thing out there. We don't need to discount it."

You: "Sorry, but it's over my budget. I'll have to think it over."

Clerk: "This is our last one. We sold our entire stock in two weeks. If you come back tomorrow, this one won't be here. You'll pay less for a different model and never stop thinking about this one. You don't want to miss your window of opportunity, do you?"

You: "Hmmm. If this one is so hot you'll order another shipment, and there are other stores that carry this computer. Can you give me a better reason why I should buy it from you today?"

Fight or flight

Fear elicits our "fight or flight" response to perceived danger. You can ask for something out of fear (fight) or run from asking and say nothing (flight). When your fear is strong enough, you protect yourself by choosing either fight or flight. Fear affects your WIFM decision-making process and all the WIFM motivations can be affected by fear.

In fight, the wrong words said in the heat of a fearful moment lead to regret, and fear induced rash behavior could come back to bite you on the butt. Fear of waiting prevents you from pausing to take a more reasoned approach to finding more appropriate words and behavior.

Example

Words said in haste:

"Wait! Don't go. I'll do anything! What do you want me to do?"

Words said after pausing to think:

"Let's both get some rest and see how we feel tomorrow. May I call you after you've had your morning coffee?"

In flight, fear keeps your tongue silenced and your behavior in check. It can make you feel undeserving, impotent, worthless, in danger, on guard, prepared to receive less, or serve to "keep you in your place." It can render you unable to take the minor risks in daily life that don't seem to concern others in similar situations. You can overcome a habit of deferred action and increase your ability to be successful. In addition, you can ask to put distance between you and a perceived fear, as shown in the next example.

Example

Instead of letting fear silence you completely, let your emotions speak.

- "I'm feeling uncomfortable right now because what you're saying is different than what I understood. If you really want to help me, you'll give me some time to verify the information. You do want to help me, don't you?"

- "I feel pushed and I don't appreciate it. Nothing's going to change between today and tomorrow. What's the rush?"

Identifying and admitting to your fears is the first step toward remedy. Common ways to help you overcome your fears are through cognitive reasoning, emotional counseling and behavior modification. There are therapists who specialize in each of these modalities. Everyone learns differently. Your personality type helps determine which learning mode is best for you. Thinking types will favor cognitive reasoning, feeling will match with an emotional modality, and sensing pairs with behavior modification. Exercises for exploring these three options are described below.

Cognitive reasoning

Analytical types can tease out the reason behind their fears, then make a decision to change their mindset to reflect the person they'd like to be. People are frequently afraid of what they don't understand. They fear the unknown. Gain an understanding and the fear dissipates.

Example

Suppose you'd like to ask your parents for a personal loan to help you get through a time of lost income due to reduced hours at work. You may not know exactly why you're afraid to ask for the money, though you have some ideas.

Write a list of your fears and make note if they still seem reasonable today as opposed to being a holdover from your formative years. Your childhood beliefs may have solidified and not evolved as you grew older. This can happen. Many children learn to be afraid of their parents and never grow out of it. Is that belief holding you back from asking for that loan?

As an adult you can legitimately question whether you still fear your parents. If you ask your parents for a loan, will they lash out in such a way that being fearful is a wise precaution? Your reaction to your parents' behavior doesn't have to be the same as your siblings, nor does it need to mimic what it was when you were a child. Challenging your belief system can be scary. As an adult you make decisions, including whether your fears still seem logically founded.

Try the exercise entitled "What if…and then…" found in the Chapter 31, *Putting Your Decision to Ask into Action*. You can talk yourself through your dilemma by asking, "What if…I asked my parents for a loan?" How do you answer? "And then…" what would you do or say next? Try a variety of approaches and listen to what you tell yourself. Your self-talk may have more to do with why you don't ask than anything you think your parents might say.

In the same chapter, review the section entitled "Pro and Con" and then write out your lists. Here are three sample pro points for asking for that loan:

- You can get current on your bills.

- You won't be as stressed out.

- Your parents loaned your sister money when she needed it.

Three con points are:

- Asking makes you feel like a failure.

- Your parents may become angry or abusive.

- Your parents may ask you to make tough financial concessions during the time of the loan.

Continue the exercise as described, writing down WIFM motivations for yourself and your parents. If you can live with the answer, you can ask the question.

Geena's father was a screamer and verbally abusive. Growing up, she remembered hearing arguments between her parents that went long into the night. As a child, she held a pillow over her head to escape the noise and learned to be careful about what she did so as not to ignite her father's ire. She moved far away as soon as she could get a job. Her parents divorced. Though infrequent, her father's visits were stressful because he bossed her around like he did when she was a girl.

Finally, Geena decided she wasn't going to put up with his every demand. She entertained the possibility that she could get more of what she wanted so the visits would be easier on her. To cope with her fear of her father, she reasoned the worst that would happen was he would yell. She decided not to cower beneath his tirade and if he decided to leave early, well, so be it.

As usual, during his visit he started ordering her around about what they would do and where they would go. She mustered her strength, and this time she turned it around. She told him what she was willing to do and gave him a couple of options. Inside she cringed, but her fear at standing up to her father was short-lived. He responded to her differently – as a grown woman capable of making decisions. From then on, she found that the more she acted like an adult around him, the more he respected her position. It was the beginning of a new relationship.

Emotional counseling

Peeling away layers of fearful emotions can leave you feeling vulnerable and at the same time it can be tremendously empowering. Don't lose touch with the fact that fears serve a purpose of self-protection. It is important to understand the line of distinction between fears that have a basis in reality and self-imposed fears that have little to do with the outside world and everything to do with you. The biggest, scariest step may be the one that leads you to ask for help. It can also be the one that transforms your life for good – a risk worth taking.

It is possible to make huge strides with assertiveness training, the right therapist or psychiatrist, a support group, or with your supportive family and friends. Those who care can help you identify your specific fears and can also be a good source to suggest options to aid in your growth.

Excessive worry and fearful thoughts may be a sign of a treatable medical condition. Consult your physician for proper advice and care. Your physician can help you determine whether medication and/or other prescribed treatments are right for you.

Behavior modification

Studies show smiling leads to happiness. Your brain is fooled. It doesn't know the difference between feeling genuine happiness and faking it. You start out not wanting to smile, you smile anyway and the next thing you know – you're smiling! Behavior modification works along similar principles. Practice a desired behavior and the next thing you know, you're making new neural pathways that form memory and new habits – the ones you want. Give yourself positive reinforcement and reward good behavior.

The exercise "Small steps" found in the Chapter 31 can be used to create changes in behavior one small step at a time. For those of you who like to ease into a swimming pool while you get used to the water, this exercise should feel more comfortable than jumping into the deep end. The next example shows you how.

Example

Suppose you want to dress better on a daily basis, but your fears of how others will react or your own fears about how you see yourself are holding you back. You know what would look better to you, but you don't put in the effort. Every time you do something to achieve your goal, give yourself a small reward to reinforce the desired behavior, e.g., you could dab on a bit of favorite cologne. When you don't take the time to dress well, you can apply negative reinforcement by not wearing that cologne or even putting on a scent you don't like. Catching a whiff of the scent during the day is an additional reminder of how you either did or didn't follow through with your goal.

Taking small steps and reinforcing behavior can be applied to many areas of your life from taking the initiative to talk to a potential date to changing eating habits for a lifetime. Support groups provide reinforcement.

Desensitize your fear

One treatment for phobias is desensitization. You do the thing you fear or you expose yourself to your fear – not all at once, but a little at a time in a controlled environment. It's a lot like taking small steps, but you may need to repeat the same action over and over on one specific area until your fear subsides. Through persistence you can progress to a point where your fear is manageable or is no longer a fear. You have one life. Don't let your personal goals go unrealized. Ask a health professional for help with debilitating fears.

For today

Important changes can seem overwhelming even when you know they are beneficial to your overall health and well-being. This is why it's helpful to remind yourself to do the behavior for the moment – for today. To press ahead into the future about how you'll ever keep up with your new regimen could seem like an impossibly scary task. Don't let yourself go there. You can make the change for one day – today. Tomorrow, repeat the lesson. The day after that, do it again.

Adriana wanted to make a few positive changes in her life. She wanted to meet new people and also decided to take up jogging. During her regular run, she met up with one of her new jogging acquaintances in search of his lost dog. She helped search and luckily, found and returned the dog. The man gave Adriana his phone number. At first, shyness kept her from calling. Determined to continue with the changes she asked of herself, she made the call. Before long, the two founded an acting group. Their friendship and years-long association led to many opportunities for Adriana and helped change the direction of her life for the better.

Act as if

You don't have to take a formal acting class to act "as if." Try acting as if you are a person who is not afraid. Take on the role of the person you'd like to be and speak the words that person would say. Act as if the beliefs you want to believe are the ones you actually do believe. Act as if the confidence you desire is already embodied within you. You can add to the character you create in other ways, such as dressing differently or enunciating your words more clearly. Do it for today. The day after that, do it again.

Practice

Pick a fear you'd like to overcome, for example, speaking up for yourself. Pair your fear with the method that suits you best: cognitive reasoning, emotional counseling, behavior modification, or tackle it head on as shown in some of the examples above. Any way you choose, take that first step to empower yourself.

Ask for More Out of Life

Not many things are given to you on a platter; you have to work for what you want. Ask yourself what is important for you to live fully. Then ask yourself how you will give yourself those things and how you can sustain their presence.

Personal goals are an inside job

No one hands you goals or achieves them for you. They are yours to earn. You also give yourself security, self-esteem, and values. Others certainly contribute, but ultimately it's an inside job. You adopt your values by what you were taught, through your understanding of life and how you feel inside at a gut level. You may feel your values are sacred, time-honored traditions worthy of respect and renewal or you might feel much of what you learned is nonsense. Self-esteem isn't given to you either. You develop it through your sense of self. As for security, the correct environment can help make you feel physically secure. It can't protect you against your doubts. You have control over yourself and if you don't like the direction your life has taken, you can retake control of your life.

Whatever goals you choose they include the motivations of WIFM – what's in it for me. To review, they are:

- Emotional
- Physical/Energy
- Logical

- Fairness

- Spiritual/Beliefs

- Personal

- Financial

Ask yourself for what you want

Requests invite involvement. As you've learned, asking *who, what, where, when, why, how* and *which* makes a difference. When you ask of yourself, you can ask the same way. Allow yourself to become involved on many levels. To do this, consider your WIFM from all aspects.

Good questions to ask yourself

- "What are my short- and long-term goals?"

- "Am I asking for what's right for me?"

- "Am I being honest with myself?"

- "Am I ready to give and receive to further the process?"

- "Am I ready to be responsible for my actions?"

- "Am I ready to accept the outcome?"

Each of these questions is discussed below.

Choose and define your goals

Many folks have vague ideas instead of focused short- and long-term goals. A defined goal is a specific desire with a set time line. A vague goal has disjointed structure and no set time line for completion. The more specific you can be, the better you will be able to connect the dots to reaching your goal.

Example

Vague: "I'd like to teach someday."

Defined: "I'd like to get my teaching certificate within three years and work at a local elementary school."

Now you can ask yourself to research universities that offer a teaching certificate. You can look into the costs and the actual time you will need to get your certificate. The more you learn, the more you will be able to fill in the missing areas of what to do until you have a fleshed out goal and the knowledge to take you there.

So many choices

It isn't always easy to know what you want for yourself. You may be able to define your goals, or you might choose to ask for help. Avail yourself of the community-at-large. Assistance is out there in the form of career counselors, life coaches, computer geniuses, mentors, psychologists, physical trainers, organizational specialists, nature clubs, school counselors, dance instructors, music teachers, doctors, free or paid classes, spiritual advisors, financial consultants, speaking groups, and more. A few sessions with one of these groups or professionals can help you form a realistic goal, and then help you find ways to achieve it. Newspapers, libraries and the Internet are great resources to find special interest groups or meet-ups in your area. Volunteer work is also known to get folks involved in areas they would not have previously considered. You don't have to know ahead of time whether you will like something. You only have to try with an open mind. The next chapter, *Goal Mining Expeditions*, offers a series of exercises to help you find worthy goals and define existing ones.

What's right for you

Practical limitations may prevent or slow your progress in reaching your goal; but that didn't stop Jim Abbott, the one-handed pitcher, from playing baseball in the 1988 Summer Olympics. We're all wired a little differently, which means your level of persistence and drive is not going to be the same as everyone else's. Recognize that everyone has setbacks, but not everyone stays back. Be kind and reward yourself in small, meaningful ways as you take steps to reach your goal. Do what you can and strive for improvement. Rewards, by their nature, are WIFM.

It's not unusual to ask another to join in a mutual goal, though your WIFM motivations may be different than your partner's. When you join with another, you may have to give up something for the sake of achieving the bigger prize. On the other hand, your partner brings in benefits you would not have without him or her.

Example

Your goal may involve pairing up with another to lose weight. When you ask to team up with the person who buys the groceries, chances are good you'll have the right foods around to help achieve your shared goal. By encouraging one another, you can accomplish more as a team than you would individually. This is called synergy.

You have control over yourself, not your teammate who might decide to stop dieting. Ask why and look to your teammate's WIFM for reasons. In the event your teammate deliberately tries to thwart your progress, again look to WIFM. You then have a decision to make about how to proceed with your goal. You may decide to buy your own groceries while deciding how to proceed with your teammate.

Be honest

Be honest with yourself. Your dreams are meant to open your eyes, not blind you to reality. To help this come about, ask yourself for clarity. Be practical, keep perspective and move your dreams outside your head and into action.

Pay attention to the little voices inside you that spur you on and issue warnings. These messages are a small part of the whole. Acknowledge their role and importance or they will arise again.

Being honest is also about choosing your goals and not living someone else's dream. Nor is it forcing your goal on another. You cannot change another person or set a goal for them, but you can encourage their participation in yours. Choosing one goal could mean letting go of another, at least temporarily. You may have to decide between being a full-time welder or a long-distance trucker because you physically cannot do both.

Give and receive

Personal goals present you with an opportunity to give and receive. Are you ready for both? You give your time and attention, and may receive the time and attention of others. You give and gain emotion, knowledge, creativity, money, and so on as you work your way toward your desired end.

Not everyone is equally adept at giving and receiving. You must allow yourself to experience both. You may need to break old patterns of behavior to effectively give and receive. It could mean changing the authoritative inner voice in your head from: "You can't do that" or, the personalized inner voice of: "I can't do that" to "I can and I will find a way."

Reaching your goal may mean learning how to say "No" to others or delegating responsibilities at home or work. As much as you would like to devote a great deal of time and energy to all your projects, family, friends, career, etc., there are only so many hours in the day. You will have the task of deciding what to cut back or cut out completely. For others, the change might be learning how to say

"Yes," to receive things, people, education, actions and feelings into their lives as part of reaching their goal.

Be responsible

Being ready for responsibility includes recognizing the difference between valid reasons out of your control and excuses that justify behavior within your control. Underachievers frequently recognize when poor behavior or lack-luster performance holds them back, even as they are busy fixing the blame, not the problem. The next time you point a finger, look in the mirror and see who's there. Then go through each WIFM category and ask yourself how your old ways fit your justifications.

Your drive and enthusiasm propel you forward. Ask yourself not only how your decisions will affect others, but how you will be different during the goal journey and at the destination.

Acceptance

When you ask for direction, you cannot know your ultimate path. Are you ready to accept unknown outcomes? You can ask for guidance along the way to stay on your path or fine-tune your goals. Only you know whether to follow your head or your heart. That trade-off may never come up, but sacrifice is surely in the cards. The longer you live, the more you realize life is short and there is limited time to accomplish your goals. You can change your priorities and even drop some goals to focus on the ones you believe will bring the greatest joy, whether you succeed to your fullest desires or not. Acceptance brings peace.

Stay on track

Inside, you feel the strength of your goal, which helps determine your desire to reach it. If the sacrifices are too great to bear all at once, you may need a long-range plan, such as saving for years to buy a tackle shop at retirement. If the sacrifices are not too great and you end up spending time hanging with your buddies instead of working toward what you say you want, ask yourself about the true strength of your goal versus your WIFM motivations. Allow yourself the freedom to take corrective action to get yourself back on track.

As a divorced working mom with school-aged kids and a house to run, Tamara had little time and resources to pursue the college degree she always wanted. Rather than give up her goal, she asked herself how she could achieve it and decided to fit in one class at a time. Tamara stuck to her plan and took three classes a year, one each semester. Years passed and she eventually received an AA degree from the local community college. She transferred to the state university system and continued on, one class at a time. She joked about being the oldest student and the student enrolled for the longest period of time. On the day she earned her Bachelor's degree no one could have been more proud, unless it was her children who watched her make it happen.

Resist the temptation to edit

Most people have a tendency to edit or filter their desires by deciding which goals are attainable based on current events. This temptation is self-defeating. Let yourself dream. Put yourself in the picture. At the start, you don't have to know how you will reach your goal. Decide on a goal, then let it evolve. Share your dream with others who will be supportive. Listen to their suggestions about how you could make it happen, no matter how crazy it might sound. Later, you may feel differently. You could work to put yourself in a position where attaining your goal is not so crazy after all. I know this is true from personal experience.

After a twelve-year break of not working, I had to begin anew and find a career. First, I asked myself what I could do that could eventually lead to a good living wage, even though I had no recent work history. After much consideration, I decided to try auto sales. Though I had no financial background, my five-year plan was to become a finance manager. After five months of persistent inquiries at one specific dealership, the sales manager took a chance on me. I applied myself and after six months on the job I was top salesperson. After one year, I bought a house, another thing I had asked of myself. Around the same time, I attended my cousin's wedding and coincidentally or not (read about manifesting in the next chapter Goal Mining Expeditions*) sat next to an auto industry recruiter who was sure I would make a talented finance manager. A year and a half after I started in auto sales I was training to be a finance manager. I wouldn't have believed it if I hadn't done it myself.*

Generally speaking, friends and family are accessible sources of information and support. You will be amazed at the wealth of knowledge and experience held by others in your circle of influence. Ask them about your particular area of interest. People who know you well are able to offer insights that would elude someone you've just met. Talk with those you respect about your desire to form and achieve your goal. Your genuine interest will generate a genuine answer. Listen to what they recommend and trust your instincts.

Practice

Think of one of your long-term goals. Break it up into manageable parts, like you did in the exercise "Small Steps," and assign a time line to each part.

Goal Mining Expeditions

Vague goals lack clarity and direction. Definition is an important step toward your true destination – the realization of your goals. Perhaps you need a goal. The following creative exercises will help you mine hidden desires buried beneath your conscious mind to help you find and/or clarify your goals. This is your golden opportunity to help you live a more valuable life.

Choosing goals

Whether you need to establish new goals or further define the ones you have, practicing right-brain exercise, meditation, guided imagery and/or manifestation techniques can help. These techniques include asking for a goal or direction. Your answer may come in the form of a feeling, a symbolic picture, action, or actual words that enter your head. You might be inclined to dismiss an unexpected answer. Allow yourself to be receptive to whatever comes in.

Too much left brain thinking, what I call "analysis paralysis," can bog you down. Right brain exercises are a great way to tap into the creative part of your mind to find answers your left brain can't effectively access.

Find a goal using imagery

A fun, creative exercise is to make a poster using cutouts from magazines for a personal dream board. Invite supportive friends or family to join you and ask them to bring extra magazines. More people can raise the energy in the room and music can stimulate creativity. Have poster board, scissors, a variety of colorful magazines and glue sticks on hand. Cut out pictures that represent your dreams – a grand piano, a vacation scene, lovers, a dog bounding in the surf, a career uniform, words from headlines, whatever you choose, and paste the pictures and messages on the board. Afterward, do a show and tell.

The intent you imagine when creating your dream board helps make it a reality. Keep the board in your bedroom or in a place where you will see it frequently. These references are a visual affirmation of your desires and goals. You can make this a private exercise and share it later if you like. Also, if it's been a long time since you've made a dream board, try it again and watch new messages emerge. Give yourself kudos for dreams realized.

Meditation

Meditation is a great way to clear the mind, opening the way to possibilities and the ability for heightened focus. Have you ever had a question before going to bed and woken up with the answer? Meditation can work the same way. Here's how to include a request as part of your meditation.

Om sweet om

Beginners find a distraction-free setting helps clear the mind. Soft, instrumental music without rhythm or words is known to aid in this process, though some prefer quiet. A drumbeat similar to a heartbeat can help you focus internally to get your meditation started and also serves as a focal point should your thoughts stray.

Form your question before beginning your meditation or at the onset. Get physically comfortable. Any style of meditation will be fine, just allow enough time, ten to fifteen minutes or more. You need not focus on your question during your session, though it may pop in at a particular moment. Allow your mind to wander or follow where it leads you. Various sounds, distractions, and thoughts about daily life are normal. Pull yourself back into your meditation by listening to the drumbeat in your CD, focusing on your breath, or repeating a mantra or single word such as "one" or "om."

Listen, watch and feel for your answer during your session. You may receive a single word, a long dissertation, a feeling, or visual response. Non-specific or symbolic messages that seem unconnected to your request might confuse you or be hard to interpret. Be open to whatever comes in. The answers you receive aren't always what you hope for or expect. Write down your experience in a journal for future reference. Answers can take time to untangle. Your response could be amazingly clear and revelatory. Ask a friend familiar with meditation or dream interpretation for their feedback and be open to how their impressions add to your own.

During meditation it may seem like nothing happens or random thoughts pervade your session. You may forget everything as soon as it is over or think you were asleep part of the time. Your conscious mind might forget, but the process continues at a deeper level. Answers have been known to arrive in a flash or "Aha!" moment when you are thinking about something else. It may take a few mediations before you are able to understand what happens. Try varying your effort, such as rewording your question. Meditation skills are honed through practice. Stay with it long enough and you'll come to realize how much you overlooked when interpreting those early efforts.

I was fortunate to have a cat for almost fifteen years. He was a sweet, loving kitty and I mourned his passing. A few days after I laid him to rest, I decided to do a meditation.

223

Instead of asking a specific question, I asked for whatever might come in related to my loss. After I closed my eyes and got settled, I saw a small square of blurred light that faded in and out. This happened a few times and then there was nothing. Suddenly, I saw a vivid scene of a dozen joyous women in a drumming circle. In a second, I snapped out of my meditation. The scene made me feel comforted. I wondered if somehow his crossing over had been guided or celebrated by these women who were unknown to me. I thought of it over the next few days and occasionally thereafter. It helped me deal with the loss of my pet.

Visualization and guided imagery

Visualization and guided imagery begin in a relaxed state and can take place during meditation. Prepare a question ahead of time to ask during your session. It is normal when you first close your eyes to see nothing in particular or fuzzy colors in random patterns. These nondescript images can take form and send you on your way. For a more structured beginning, think of a place where you feel relaxed and imagine being there. Or, listen to a friend's guided direction to take you to a place in nature where you feel safe. There are many CD's and DVD's designed to talk you through this process. On your own, variations to this exercise are limited only by your imagination.

Take a little trip

After relaxing and with eyes closed, visually journey in your mind's eye following your own path or by listening to the guidance of another who helps you roam into an experiential realm. Many people like to imagine being in a natural environment. At a set point, you may encounter guides or others to whom you may ask your question. Ask aloud or silently transmit your request. You can address your request to no one in particular or to the surrounding elements. Your individual journey may deviate from the suggestions given to you and you may find yourself far from where you thought you would end up going. This is part of the process. Go with it. As with meditation, your answer may take any sensory form. When the session concludes, you may wish to share your journey with others or write down the experience in a journal.

As a co-facilitator at a smoking cessation clinic, I led the participants in a guided imagery session. I had them journey out of the city into a green and sweet-smelling meadow. In the center of the meadow was a hot air balloon. I suggested they put something into the basket at the base of the balloon and made sure to give them enough time for whatever it was they had to give away. The strings of the balloon were cut and the basket with its contents floated up into the sky. It became smaller and smaller and then disappeared.

Afterward, we shared stories. Several participants loaded up the balloon with cigarette packs. One woman tossed in every cigarette she imagined smoking in her entire life and comically explained how the basket was loaded. Others heaved in all sorts of excess baggage from their lives that seemingly had nothing to do with smoking. All found the exercise helpful.

Meditation and guided imagery have gained in popularity and are considered mainstream treatments for stress reduction. Meditation is like a form of self-hypnosis, which has proved helpful for those trying to attain specific personal goals. There are other less-used modalities out there. Perhaps you have heard of them or even tried them for yourself.

Dreamwork

As mentioned, sleep and dreams can aid in problem solving. You can take an active role by working with your dreams. Treat your nighttime adventures much the same as during meditation and guided imagery, including inviting spiritual entities to join you before you go to sleep. Dreamtime has long been recognized as a potential doorway through which God, spirits and others have appeared or spoken. You may ask questions during lucid dreaming or hear yourself ask for something in a dream you find startling. Dreams aren't just for replaying a symbolic version of your recent past. They are a portal to your inner psyche.

Active dreaming

You can begin by focusing on your question before you fall asleep. Devote a moment of concentration on whomever or whatever you would like to see in your dream. Keep a journal by your bed to record what transpires as details have a way of disappearing shortly after waking. Don't decide upon waking whether insignificant details are worthy of your attention. Write everything down including colors, smells, sounds, conversation, people, animals, environment, feelings, action and anything else you sense or interpret. You will be able to review your notes and make further connections when you're awake without guessing about what happened. The words you choose to describe your experience can be key determinants to what transpired.

You can train yourself to wake up after a dream. Not everyone is successful when it comes to remembering, but that doesn't mean the work isn't getting done. Thoughts and ideas stimulated from your dreams may come to you during waking moments. You may not be aware how the dream process aided your request.

Those who practice lucid dreaming are able to control events as they occur during the dream. Imagine being able to bring in whomever you choose into your dream and then being able to ask your question.

A few years ago, Carlos was working sporadically and was showing early signs of depression. He was unhappy with the options available to him and felt he was floundering. During a meditation, he asked for guides to help him. Nothing came during the meditation. Two evenings later he had a dream. In it, a large hawk about twenty-five feet tall was perched in a nearby tree. The hawk swooped down and Carlos thought he was about to become a meal for this giant predator. It landed on the ground nearby and stood guard. It became clear the bird was there for his protection. He sensed it was a grandfather, an ancestor in hawk form. He woke up and felt relief knowing that someone was watching over him.

Manifesting

Manifesting is a word used to describe a way to bring in material and nonmaterial desires. Messages are sent out to the universe, to a guide or guides, spirits, or to no one in particular. You can ask things for yourself or others. The idea is to focus on your thoughts or the desired outcome or object. It isn't important to know how it will come your way. Sending out messages to the universe with sincerity and intent is all it takes. Some call this focused energy the "Law of Attraction."

Add to the pot

A manifestation pot is a special container meant to hold representations of your desire. You may choose a fabric-covered box, a painted gourd, or make your own container. Each time you place something inside you will be doing so with a wish for manifesting. For example, place a quarter in the pot and say or think about increasing your income or maybe gathering more coins from different sources to give to charity. For those seeking artistic inspiration, drop in a crayon, pen or pencil; for more time in nature put in a feather or stone. You can ascribe any meaning to any object. You can blow your wish onto the object or speak your request out loud. These efforts help you focus your desire and give you an opportunity to speak your request.

> For her manifestation pot, Olivia decorated a gourd with beads and metallic paint. She placed it on a coffee table and added to it all year. She tossed in coins and paper money (for wealth), a pencil (for writing), a marble (for fun) and so on. Near the end of the year, and having achieved much of what she asked for, she felt it was time to reassess the contents. But before Olivia could go through the contents the pot split open, as if confirming her thoughts that it was time.

Practice

For the creative among you, choose a visualization or right-brain exercise to explore a creative aspect of your chosen goal or to help you form a goal. Logical types can pick apart their goal using a pros and cons approach. For a real challenge, choose a method other than the one to which you are naturally inclined.

Making the Right Request

"Be careful what you ask for – you might get it," is a cautionary phrase of untold possibilities. Getting what you want is a good thing, right? And yet, it sounds ominous.

Unintended and unanticipated consequences

You asked for a promotion and now you're away more than you're home. Your new house with the big garden takes more work than you ever imagined, leaving you no time to enjoy it. The classic sports car you wanted so badly is in the shop more than on the road. Initial pleasure from getting what you want has reversed course. You've spun 180 degrees and looking back, you wonder how it happened.

Face it, you want what you want. You're told, "Keep your eye on the prize." You think positive thoughts, repel negativity, and dream of your heart's desire. You work hard to achieve your goal, and get other things you would not have wished for in the bargain.

"I didn't ask for this."

Why didn't things turn out the way you expected? It's possible:

- You asked for the wrong thing.

- Tunnel vision kept you from seeing the bigger picture.

- Denial prevented you from accepting the consequences of your desire.

These points speak to lack of preparation in making an informed decision as well as the emphasis of desirable WIFM motivations at the expense of others you wish weren't there.

Asking for what you really want

You may think you know what you want in a broad sense. Being nonspecific can inadvertently send you off in the wrong direction. Add in important details to help figure out what you really want before you launch your quest.

Rachel worked in an office, belonged to social groups and had a busy, happy life with one exception – no husband. She had been in several long-term relationships with men who had no interest in marriage. Her friends were married with children. Rachel wanted children, too, and her biological clock was ticking. Thoughts of wedding showers, her beautiful white gown and wedding day filled her mind. She put her efforts into finding a man who wanted to marry and found one. After a short romance, he proposed and she accepted.

Her delight was palpable to her friends and family who could not totally embrace her joy for they could also see what she could not; the only thing the couple shared in common was their desire to be married. It was a terrible match. She ignored warnings from her friends and family, preferring to believe she had gotten what she wanted.

Rachel's singular focus continued beyond her wedding shower, and as time passed problems arose between her and her fiancé. During an extended trip together the time alone compounded their differences, and being away from familiar support systems forced Rachel to face a difficult realization, she had asked for the wrong thing (a man who wanted to marry) and got it. She canceled the engagement. Rachel shifted her focus off the fairy tale marriage day and onto what an actual marriage would be like. Shortly thereafter, she was introduced to the man she eventually married.

Light at the end of the tunnel

Your goal is like the light at the end of the tunnel. You may be intently focused to the point where anything on the sidelines is a blur. Warning signs are posted by the edge of the road, even in a tunnel. Your warning signs are there, too, but you have to look at them. Otherwise, you could miss an important message as you whiz on by. Often times, goals are not achieved in a straight shot for a reason. Pay attention to the signs that come into view. Take in the ambience and gather what you need along the way.

After his brief marriage broke up, Dennis, 23, rented a spacious two-bedroom unit in his old neighborhood. Living alone for a year allowed him to get his life back on track. He reconnected with old friends, including Zach, a high school buddy still living with his mom. Dennis encouraged Zach to get out from under his mother's protective wing by asking his friend to move into the spare room. Zach was reluctant, but Dennis pushed because he wanted the extra rent money and he thought the two would have fun being housemates. After more convincing, Zach agreed.

Within weeks of the move, the arrangement turned sour. Instead of having fun, the two argued over seemingly small issues. Dennis dismissed a red flag – Zach was not mature enough to be out on his own and that was why he lived with his mother. Zach showed his resentment by exhibiting passive-aggressive and childish behavior. Angry over Zach's hostility and immaturity, Dennis took a job in another area and moved out. Their friendship never recovered.

Denial is a temporary convenience

Some folks are blissfully unobservant of their surroundings, while others are firmly in denial. Denial can be used as a delaying tactic. It's a way of fooling yourself into believing there are no red flags. It allows you to focus on what you want without the distraction of inconvenient or troublesome issues or realities getting in the way. Denial can be self-protective, however, the truth has a way of coming out.

Prepare for the unexpected

Learned economists can't seem to agree on what the future holds and they've spent entire careers studying trends and numbers. Life may be a mystery with the future unknown, but you can still plan ahead. The techniques you've learned thus far can be used to help you see the signs along the road to your success. The more you share your ideas with others, the more opportunity you have to learn about what to watch for along the way. Your support systems can help you define and refine your goal, so you ask for the right thing.

When getting what you want feels likes like a double-edged sword, you'll wonder what went wrong. Don't set yourself up for disappointment. Be proactive. After you've set your goal, ask yourself these seldom-asked questions:

- Are you focusing on the right subject?
- When you think about acquiring, do you also consider what you need to give up?
- Can you add to your load without compromising the status quo of things you want to keep?

- Does your request include aspects out of your control, such as the behavior and beliefs of others?

- Are you using your desire to cover up denial of a larger issue?

- Are you willing to identify all aspects of your request and their potential effect on others?

Your honest answer to these questions can make a difference. Limit unanticipated and unintended consequences from entering the picture and dampening your initial joy from getting your wish.

Failing your way to success

No one gets everything they want even when they believe they asked the right way. Don't give in to perceived failure. Give yourself permission to think of the experience as an opportunity to learn and you will have failed at nothing. There may be legitimate reasons why you didn't get what you want. Your excuses, on the other hand, are justifications for things not going your way. Instead of making excuses, next time ask yourself what you would do differently.

Everyone makes mistakes and you will make your share. It's okay. They help guide your way. One mistake you need never make is to keep yourself tightly constrained so that you can never make any mistakes at all.

Your ability to see options, to find solutions and act upon them is what turns a failure into a possibility, and a possibility into an opportunity for success. Each time you review and apply the information, techniques and tips contained in *You Don't Ask, You Don't Get*, you will reinforce how to ask for what you want and increase your chances for success.

Learn from the actions of others

You will have plenty of company with others trying to get what they want. After reading this book it will be easier for you to see the reasons why others fall short. Listen to what they say and do, or don't say and do, and consider how they could improve their lot by using the techniques you've learned. I encourage you to share this information. You will help others and help yourself at the same time.

You Don't Ask, You Don't Get gives you the knowledge you need and the tools to put that knowledge into action. Through practice, you will gain confidence as you learn from your mistakes and from your successes. You can get what you want; all you have to do is ask!

You don't ask, you don't get

Now you know – make the right request, learn from your mistakes and try again. You could get exactly what you want. Let yourself believe you can get what you want. That's what happened to the woman in this next story.

As a practicing minister, Cecilia knew many of the residents in the small northern California town she called home. The nice house she rented was very private, but too pricey for her to continue living there alone. Her numerous contacts would have made it easy to find a roommate to share expenses. Instead, she decided to go to an agency and ask for what she really wanted, a roommate who would rarely be there so she could continue to enjoy her privacy as much as possible. The agency found a man who needed residency in her neighborhood, but who frequently traveled for business and would rarely be there. It was a perfect arrangement.

Practice

Think of a goal you are currently working on. Do you think you asked for the right thing? When you consider the warning signs, can you connect them to WIFM motivations? Is there a WIFM motivation overpowering others that could work toward your detriment?

Empower Your Personal Relationships

How do you get what you want from your relationships? The same way you ask for anything else – by appealing to the other person's WIFM using the techniques shown in this book. Remember, you can't change others, but you can find an incentive for them to see things your way. Find their motivations and connect them to your desires.

What do men/women want?

Let's get this question out of the way right now. The reason you keep asking this is because you can't get a satisfactory answer, and you can't get a satisfactory answer because *it's the wrong question!* You can't lump half the population together and expect a specific answer. For the most part, what men and women want is to be loved and appreciated for the unique individuals they are, as well as to be treated with kindness and respect. Repeat this mantra: "My friend/lover/partner/spouse is a unique individual." And don't you feel the same? Believe it and act accordingly. Voila! No more mystery.

What do you ask?

In an attempt to further your personal relationships, you'll want to share information about yourself. That's great, but only half the equation. Invite others to share by asking questions about them. Conversation will flow from this exchange. What do you ask?

- Ask questions that invite involvement.

- Ask questions meant to show your feelings and consideration for the other person.

- Ask questions in a positive tone.

- Ask questions that demonstrate your interest in the other person and your relationship.

Example

- "I hear you're talking a class. Why did you choose it and what are you learning?"

- "Reunions can be boring when you don't know anyone. My family is excited you're coming. How can I make this an enjoyable visit for you?"

- "You look great! How have you been spending your time?"

Things don't always go your way in relationships. Familiarity can end up being an excuse for an inconsiderate attitude. When it's your turn to talk, explain your feelings using "I" statements. Give the other person the benefit of the doubt and try to keep a positive tone. Accusations prompt others to respond defensively. They may take the offensive and come out with some accusations of their own. Your positive approach can head off this type of scenario before it gets started.

Example

Not you: "Why won't you spend more time with me?"

You: "I'd like to spend more time together. You're planning to go fishing this Saturday, right? May I join you?"

Not you: "Don't you have anything better to do than lie around in your bathrobe?"

You: "Let's do something fun today. If you could choose anything, what would it be?"

238

The strength of WIFM binds you with another. Your motivations don't have to be identical and neither do the strength of your feelings for one another. In an adult/adult give-and-take relationship you may give one thing and get something completely different. You have free will that enables you and others to agree or disagree, to connect and break-up, and to ask and respond in the way you see fit. The adult/minor child relationship has a different dynamic because the child depends on the adult for nurture, sustenance, guidance and authority.

Amber and Danita were friends in junior high school. Fifteen years later, both moved to California where they renewed their friendship as adults. They had fun bar hopping and looking for guys. Amber began a relationship with a man and moved in with him. She still enjoyed seeing Danita, but Danita didn't seem as interested even though she had no problem with Amber's new boyfriend. Amber didn't understand why Danita was being standoffish. After all, wasn't getting a boyfriend their shared goal? Hadn't they had fun?

When Amber and her boyfriend invited Danita to a party at their house, Danita asked if any single guys would be there. The reply didn't spark Danita's interest and she declined the invitation. Amber realized what she wanted from Danita was different from what Danita wanted from her. It was likely Danita realized the same thing, because from that moment on neither one contacted the other.

By inviting Danita to a party, Amber was asking for her continued friendship. For Danita, their friendship was merely the means to her stronger, personal goal of finding a boyfriend. Since Amber was no longer able to help Danita reach her personal goal, the emotional WIFM of the friendship was not strong enough on its own – at least from Danita's point of view – to carry the relationship forward.

The impossible dream

Always remember – you are in charge of yourself, your feelings and actions. You may influence others, but it is up to them to be who they will be. You cannot change anyone's personality or make them quit habits because you ask them. Change comes from within. To be persuasive, you must tap into the other person's WIFM motivations at a deep level. Only then might they adopt your point of view over their own. You can't force any of your WIFM motivations onto another.

Example

Not you: "Will you quit smoking/drinking/overeating for me?"

You: "I care about you. I'm wondering what it'll take for you to pay attention to your health. Will you look at this clinic brochure?"

Not you: "Your idea for this business is a disaster waiting to happen. Why aren't you listening to me?"

You: "I understand your concern. I want to improve our finances, too. We need to find a business that doesn't sacrifice everything we've already worked for. There are no guarantees. Personally, I couldn't work under that kind of stress. Could you?"

Listen for expectations

Expectation is evident when you hear the words *should* or *ought*. Thinking along these lines is a good indication you are only listening to your own WIFM motivations. You know what you want because you think, feel and hear your own self-talk. No one is a mind reader. Some people are naturally more perceptive than others or more interested in pleasing another. They pick up on clues that others miss or ignore.

Example

Not you: "Why am I angry? Don't you think you should know by now?"

You: "I'm angry because you forgot our anniversary. It's important to me. Isn't it important to you, too?"

Everyone thinks, feels and relates slightly different from everyone else, and people's actions follow their own reasons. You can't make another person wrong, but how you speak can prompt defensive reactions.

Not you: "It's all your fault! How could you?"

You: "I'm very upset! This is not how we agreed to handle things. Did something change since we talked?"

Stay true to your integrity

Your personal desire to please another may drive you to meet that person's expectations. You must ask yourself whether you are being true to yourself during this process. Most of us are willing to overlook small sacrifices, that is, to take a small step away from our comfort range. A large step could be a growth experience. It could also leave you asking: "Why did I let myself get talked into this?" Stay true to your integrity and you won't worry about not meeting the expectations of others.

Your values are important. They are tied to your beliefs. Remember this when you are trying to talk someone into doing something for you. Their resistance tells you their WIFM motivations are not the same as yours.

Can you both get enough of what you want?

Relationships are complex and immensely rewarding, which is why you keep working at them. You know what happens when the WIFM payoff falls below an acceptable level; the relationship deteriorates. Couples with too many conflicting motivations find it difficult to sustain a relationship at a satisfactory level. When a couple shares motivations and still can't get along, sessions with a counselor can prove effective in identifying unrecognized areas of conflict.

Motivations can be ingrained to the point where WIFM does not seem like a choice. Your rigid stance or deeply held conviction leaves little or no grey area for the differences of others. Conversely, loosely held beliefs and modes of behavior can make you vulnerable to the whims of the moment. You may feel your personality has become lost or overshadowed after following someone else's desires. Ask yourself what you want from your relationships and if you are getting enough of what you need to keep going forward.

The high divorce rate proves how difficult it is to sustain a marriage. The next story sheds light on how conflicting WIFM motivations influenced the course of a relationship.

Rosa and her young children joined as a family with Tony, whose older child lived with his mother. Tony was a strict disciplinarian, not with his own child, but with Rosa's kids. Rosa felt his style was too harsh and compensated by being softer with them than when she had been the sole parent. Rosa's son acted out, which escalated the situation. Rosa asked Tony to be less strict with her son, but Tony stood by his convictions. She then asked for family counseling. Again, he resisted, arguing that the son was the problem. Several years passed before he finally agreed to go. Their effort to create a united front as parents was impossible with both pointing fingers at the other. By then the damage had been done. Even though other areas of their relationship were intact and working, the strength of their differing beliefs prevented them from reaching a compromise. Rosa felt her primary WIFM was her duty to raise her children in a manner she saw fit. The marriage ended.

Raising children is frequently a source of conflict, as is religion, finances, politics, sex, and problems with in-laws. Establishing commonality for daily living, as well as goals, and agreeing on the means to get there helps build a strong relationship. Ask the right questions of a potential mate before you become emotionally and/or physically involved. Then, you may choose to avoid further involvement, or if you do proceed, you will be doing so with your eyes open.

Spread the word

Getting what you want might be within the power of someone you know. Initial attempts using personal relationships to get what you want don't always lead to success, but that doesn't mean your request is unattainable. You can't possibly know everything your friends know or who they know. You know even less about acquaintances.

While taking a class in foot reflexology, Charles was asked by his classmate Lisa if he knew anyone who could help her make a brochure. She was surprised when Charles said he could help her. The only thing Lisa knew about Charles was his interest in holistic health and nothing about his graphics background. It worked out well for both of them.

Oldies, but goodies

Older contacts can be invaluable. Don't assume a long period of silence means you're disconnected forever. Classmates enjoy reunions, and they don't have to be structured in ten-year intervals. Social networking sites make reconnecting easier than ever before.

As a young woman, Annie moved to California from the Midwest. Almost thirty years later, her father, who lived alone in the family home, became confused, took an overdose of his medicine and ended up in the hospital. His prognosis was grim and she flew out to see him. To make matters worse, his will and medical power-of-attorney were horribly out of date. Her father asked for her help. Fortunately, his health improved and during his recovery Annie located two friends from high school. One gave her the name of an attorney, who subsequently recommended an associate of his to quickly assist with updating her father's legal papers. Within two days, the other school friend repaired the heating system in the family home and replaced a defective stove. When her father came home from the hospital, Annie was able to fly back to California where she finished the legal details long-distance. Annie and her father were both relieved and grateful.

Six degrees of separation

When you can't locate the right person to help you get what you want, someone you know may know. Got that? The only way to find out is to ask. Whom do you ask? Everyone you know.

You'll have a much better shot at success with a network spreading the word. The last thing you want to hear is how a friend of a friend got a great deal on a used kayak when yours is tied to the garage rafters covered with cobwebs.

Friends can give you an introduction to someone they know. Here's how to go about introducing yourself by phone and making a request to someone you've never met.

Example

You: "Hello. May I please speak to Matt Smith?"

M.S.: "Speaking."

You: "Hi. My name is _____. Our mutual friend Nancy Collins suggested I call you."

M.S.: "Oh, yes, Nancy and I go way back."

You: "Great! Here's why I'm calling. I volunteer at the community theater and we're rehearsing for the upcoming show *Mystery at the Cabin*. I ran into Nancy and mentioned that I thought a stuffed deer would add character to the set and she said you have an old moose head stored in your basement. Do you think we could borrow it for the run of the show?"

Follow up

Contact those who know about your desire and remind them you are still looking. Have they heard anything? People are busy and it's easy to forget. Likewise, let them know if your search has concluded or changed. Be sure to thank them for their efforts.

Don't stop believing

Your request may be directed toward an entity: your Lord, God, Goddess, the powers that be, saints, animals, Spirit, mother earth, ancestors, guides, the universe, and so on. Prayers, ceremony, and blessings are spiritual ways to ask for things. It's a way to exercise your personal relationship with whomever or whatever you believe is out there.

It can be a challenge when for reasons unknown to you, the answer to your prayer isn't the one you hoped to get. That takes faith and acceptance. It's not unusual to desire a specific outcome for your prayer. Try asking for the greater good, that is, the outcome will be in the best interest of those involved as opposed to what you think you want.

Multiply the message

Consider group prayer for your positive outcome. Your group may choose to pray at the same time and place, or your community may be spread over the globe sending prayer at no special time and to no one specific higher entity, yet for a specified request or goal.

> When Dee's friend, Marsha, was scheduled for a difficult surgery, Dee wanted to do something for her friend who lived over two thousand miles away in Alaska. Dee suggested having a group pray for Marsha's recovery. The prayer idea appealed to Marsha, so Dee asked the group members to put out the word and have others pray for her friend. The prayers continued during the surgery and shortly thereafter. Marsha was delighted! Her recovery time was much less than what she had been told to expect. Knowing that others were praying gave Marsha great comfort, which also may have contributed to her speedy recovery.

Psychic Phenomena

The mystery surrounding psychics has prevailed through our current information and technology age. Police departments generate press when they employ a psychic to help with a stubborn case. On the other hand, telephone psychics on 900 lines have done little to elevate this practice beyond entertainment status. You may decide your personal relationship with a sensitive individual provides you with the answers to your questions, or it might be decided for you.

One day Phil and Becky were walking down the street when a woman they didn't know approached Phil. She told him that she felt compelled to tell him that the specific problem they were having with their son, which she correctly identified, was about to resolve itself. It turned out to be true.

It's in the stars

For centuries, people have looked to the heavens for answers concerning their earth-bound lives. The twelve signs of the zodiac in concert with other planetary forces give trained astrologers the information they need to interpret which forces are prevalent and how they will affect outcomes. Certain cultures still rely on the advice of astrologers to help determine everything from compatible love matches to the timing of important business decisions. You may also benefit from your personal relationship with your astrologer.

Practice

Ask yourself what you'd like more of in your personal relationships. How might you approach conversations to convey your wishes? If what you want is not within your control, how might you influence your friends and family to see your point or relate to your feelings using their WIFM motivations?

Volunteer

When it comes to self-empowerment, one of the best things you can ask for yourself is what you can do for others. Volunteer work is the epitome of giving freely. Helping others makes you feel better. There are many needy people, animals and worthwhile organizations waiting for you. Your contribution, even a very small one, is a great benefit to them. Come as you are and don't concern yourself with your level of expertise.

Meet Irv. He made wise career choices and retired at fifty. That doesn't mean he sits around doing nothing. A chunk of his time is filled encouraging others to donate to his favorite charitable organization, a group that helps children with their cancer treatments. He doesn't let economic pressures slow down donations. He asks, prods, jokes around and does what he can to let others know he's determined to keep the level of giving up where it belongs, in pace with the children in need. His cheerful attitude and persistent nature help him reach his goal. Irv feels blessed. His reward is the benefit the children receive.

Something for everyone

Bobbi plays with cats at the animal shelter. Glenn has donated gallons of blood over the years and Emily donates platelets. Jeanette made a foamcore model of gallery space her arts center uses for designing upcoming shows. Melodie and Alice shop for and deliver dry goods to an abused women's shelter. C.J. donates his time and expertise to his college alumni association. Shanice rescues injured wild birds and takes them to the animal hospital. Karina got her cartooning club involved in a Make-A-Wish fundraiser. Her husband maintains the club's website. What will you do?

Whatever it is, you will get support and encouragement whether you help a senior center with Bingo, walk a pound dog, serve meals to the homeless, help backstage at your child's dance concert or create a database for your local historical society. In the process you could gain valuable skills to put on your resume. You will meet people who share your interests and you will expand your horizons by meeting people you originally thought were the polar opposite from you.

You will not be paid in cash, but the rewards are enormous. Volunteering can provide structure in your life, a sense of well-being, pride, humility, patience and other benefits. It can build your confidence level and help change negative self-talk into positive feelings and actions that spill into other aspects of your life. Ask around and you'll find plenty of opportunities. To start, pick one that matches one or more of your WIFM motivations.

> *Lynette, a healthy, but out of shape woman on the verge of middle-age worked full-time and planned to teach an evening class between January and June. The class was cancelled and she found herself with an open block of time on her hands. While sitting in her doctor's waiting area, she picked up a brochure on Team in Training, a group committed to raising money for the Leukemia and Lymphoma Society. All she had to do was learn how to run a marathon and raise $3,500.00. What!?*

The brochure stated their support group would get her on her feet and running – a prospect that appealed to Lynette who had run short distances in high school. Plus, her mom was currently in remission with lymphoma. It seemed like a good way for Lynette to get into shape while helping a cause close to her heart. Personally, Lynette felt ready for a challenge with a beginning and a definite end, which would be a change from her habit of starting projects and not finishing them.

Lynette attended a meeting and decided to start the program. She ran with the group and by herself, carefully following the proscribed running regimen. The group explained the importance of good equipment and proper fit of her running shoes. Lynette learned how to eat special foods to keep her energy going while running long distance. Before long, she increased her mileage from a few miles to five miles to seven, ten and beyond.

In the meantime, to raise funds she followed the advice on the Team in Training web site. It was hard asking for money, but she crafted what she hoped would be a fun letter and sent it to her friends and family. Many companies have a donation match program that helped build her total and one company quadrupled a $200 donation. Lynette sought out unusual ways to raise money including making lunch for co-workers who paid for her home-cooked meals. At the end she was able to raise $7,200, more than double the amount needed.

Lynette dropped weight and gained energy, stamina and a feeling of renewal. Several months into the training she ran a half-marathon. Near the end of training she had to move and felt badly about missing her final run, the one that could prove she would be able to finish the upcoming marathon. Despite this setback, she was convinced she could do it, even if she walked over the finish line.

Her marathon was held in Anchorage, Alaska. Prepared and ready, Lynette set out on her first marathon, six months from the time she sat in the doctor's waiting area. No longer fatigued or out of shape, she alternately ran and walked the entire marathon until she sprinted the last two miles to cross the finish line.

Lynette's choice more than satisfied her WIFM motivations through volunteering. The feeling she got from sprinting across the finish line made her feel like she could accomplish anything she set her mind to. During the fundraising portion, her donors shared their stories with her, which made her feel connected and more supported than she had ever felt in her life. Lynette sustains the personal rewards she receives by continuing her volunteer efforts at various organizations.

Practice

You can be like Lynette, or Irv, or C.J., and be a hero in your own life. Take part in a bone marrow drive, stuff envelopes, make phone calls or bring a pie to your local volunteer fire department. How you ask to make a difference is your call. Just make the call.

You Can Do It

Congratulations! You've taken a huge step toward getting more out of life. You've learned why you ask for what you want, how to prompt others to give you what you want, ways to ask, how to overcome objections – both yours and others, and how to ask for all kinds of things you never thought possible. It's likely you have already had a chance to use this information to better your life and the lives of your loved ones. You asked for it and you can do it!

Reread sections of *You Don't Ask, You Don't Get* any time you wish to reinforce or add to your asking repertoire. Try some variations you may have originally passed over during your first reading. The more you exercise the tips and techniques contained in this book, the more comfortable you will feel utilizing your new skills. Before you know it, you will experience abundance coming into your life naturally and effortlessly. Giving and receiving never felt so good!

Once you've experienced benefits from practicing your new skills, please write me your successful story of self-enrichment, moment of clarity or testimonial. It could be included in a future edition to share with others so they too may find a path to a more enjoyable, rewarding life.

About the Author

Janet F. Williams

Sales professional, business owner, health consultant, writer, trainer and coach are only a few areas of expertise Janet F. Williams brings together in *You Don't Ask, You Don't Get*. She has earned a bachelor's degree in psychology and a master's degree in health education.

Janet has authored both fiction and nonfiction articles and stories. Her work has appeared in newspapers, magazines, newsletters, sales materials, books and workbooks in print and on the web. She is available for author talks.

You may contact Janet through Good Day Media.
www.GoodDayMedia.com
Info@GoodDayMedia.com

Good Day Media
P. O. Box 1007
San Marcos, CA 92079

Please visit Janet's web site at:
www.janetfwilliams.com
Blog comments welcome.